Praise for *Likeonomics*

"*Likeonomics* offers a clear path to boosting your believability, which is the secret to sales and marketing success. The premise of the book is scientifically sound: People reciprocate, especially when we elicit their emotions. Great stories, clear tips and a strong point-of-view make this a rich read."

—Tim Sanders,
author of *The Likeability Factor* and
former Chief Solutions Officer at Yahoo!

"*Likeonomics* shows us that you have to be liked to be trusted. And trust me, you are going to like—really like—this book."

—Ed Keller,
author of *The Face to Face Book* and *The Influentials*
and CEO of the Keller Fay Group

"To succeed in business you need to be more than nice, you need to be likeable—and those are two different things. *Likeonomics* offers a simple premise which I LOVE—that your ability to build strong relationships is the real path to prosperity and happiness."

—Linda Kaplan Thaler,
CEO of the Kaplan Thaler Group
and author of *The Power of Nice*

"A fascinating look at the unexpected science and power of likeability to sway our beliefs and decision making. I loved the idea behind this book!"

—Ori Brafman,
coauthor of *Sway and Click*

"Want to build a business that customers can't wait to refer to others or that employees love to work for? This is the book for you."

—John Jantsch,
small business marketing expert and author of
Duct Tape Marketing and *The Referral Engine*

"It's true. Likeability matters. Rohit Bhargava brilliantly and succinctly explains why likeability and authenticity are central to creating a trustworthy brand. In a cynical world where people are looking for things and individuals they can believe in, *Likeonomics* is a roadmap for growing your business."

—Karen Kerrigan,
President, Small Business and
Entrepreneurship Council

"Having sat through hundreds of pitch meetings, I can tell you one thing for sure . . . unlikeable entrepreneurs never get funded. In business and in life, the people who enchant us are the ones who get our attention. If you want to be among the rare few who manage to do it, read this book!"

—Guy Kawasaki,
author of *Enchantment*

"The simple but powerful stories in this book prove that values like truth, relevance, and timing matter far more than the hard sell and the seductive lure of data. We need these precepts to bring humanity back to a business world that has forgotten it."

—Josh Bernoff,
co-author of *Groundswell: Winning in a World Transformed by Social Technologies* and *Empowered: Unleash Your Employees, Energize Your Customers, and Transform Your Business*

"Finally a book that gets to the heart of why likeability is so important for both relationships and branding. Rohit Bhargava's book *Likeonomics* is a great read with well defined principles, interesting case histories and insights that uncover what really drives customer and relationship loyalty."

—Porter Gale,
former VP of Marketing for Virgin America and author of *Your Network Is Your Net Worth*

"Likeability is the new currency for success. Grounded in both research and experience, Rohit shares practical insights that will stand the test of time. *Likeonomics* is a must read that will forever change the way business is conducted."

—Gautam Gulati, MD, MBA, MPH,
Chief Medical Officer & SVP Product Management, Physicians Interactive and Adjunct Professor of Medical Innovation and Entrepreneurship, Johns Hopkins Carey Business School

"Rohit Bhargava has it right with *Likeonomics*! There are more currencies than just money and time. Building real trust involves creating a personal connection with your employees and your customers, and this book will show you how. Pay attention to *Likeonomics* and profit from being more believable than your competition."

—Chris Brogan,
President of Human Business Works and *New York Times* bestselling author of *Trust Agents*

"Rohit has hit the nail squarely on the head in terms of showing how we can better work with others to improve our chances of success in all that we do. He demonstrates through real-world examples why being liked is so critically important. 'Likeability' in the public affairs community, whether military or civilian, is critical to one's success. If you can't work and play well with others, no matter what your credentials, the results you hope to achieve will often be beyond your grasp."

—Kevin V. Arata,
Colonel, U.S. Army[*]
[*] *The views expressed are my own and do not reflect the official policy or position of the United States Army, Department of Defense, or the U.S. Government.*

"*Likeonomics* explains the importance of great relationships and building long-lasting, enduring brands."

—Tony Hsieh,
New York Times bestselling author of *Delivering Happiness*, and CEO of Zappos.com.

"In this highly entertaining book, Rohit Bhargava proves just how important being likeable is to making a compelling argument. For anyone who needs to be persuasive, deliver a great presentation, or just inspire anyone else—*Likeonomics* will help you do it."

—Nancy Duarte,
CEO of Duarte, and author of *Slide:ology* and *Resonate*

"*Likeonomics* is a wake-up call to companies and customers that the critical new business currency is brand likeability. Using insightful stories and case studies, Bhargava explains how your brand uses truth to earn trust, leverages relevance to inspire loyalty, and fosters meaningful relationships to create the most powerful competitive advantage today—likeability."

—Simon Mainwaring,
author of *New York Times* bestseller *We First*

"Every once in awhile a book comes along and changes everything. *Likeonomics* is that book. Rohit Bhargava is a modern day Dale Carnegie, in that he has pinned a new personal development classic. I will now replace my annual read *How to Win Friends and Influence People* with *Likeonomics*."

—JB Glossinger
founder of MorningCoach.com
(#1 Rated Self-Help Podcast on iTunes)

For too many of us, there is a gap between what we do and what we dream of doing. It doesn't have to be this way. For anyone who wants to close this gap of intent and really achieve your dreams, *Likeonomics* can help you get there!

—Mallika Chopra,
founder of Intent.com

Likeonomics finally puts into words so many of the things I have done to build my company from the ground up. The book itself is a case study in what Rohit preaches; he is believable, honest, relevant, and of course, likeable! His focus on storytelling instead of just theorizing makes *Likeonomics* one of the most readable business books out there.

—Scott Jordan,
CEO and founder of ScotteVest

If there is one professional fact of life, it is that having strong technical skills will only get you so far in your career. In order to boost your personal brand and make a name for yourself, you need to be likeable. If you want to build a winning career or business, then you need to read *Likeonomics*. In it, Rohit shares the truth about how likeability, unselfishness and trust are the real keys to success!

—Dan Schawbel,
personal branding guru and
Managing Partner of Millennial Branding

At the first skim of the table of contents, I was intrigued . . . but after reading *Likeonomics*, I was hooked! This book offers the rare combination of a highly practical primer filled with real world ideas for how to succeed in building your business, along with step by step guide to building trusted relationships in any situation.

—Ann Handley,
Chief Content Officer—MarketingProfs
and author of *Content Rules*

"At multiple points throughout life, your ability to build a meaningful relationship will make all the difference. From the quiet student in your chemistry class, to the cheerleader you admire from the sidelines, to the co-worker on your project, to the ideal prospect you are meeting for lunch, to the boss who will decide whether or not you get a raise—regardless of your situation, you need to be likeable. Rohit's masterful book *Likeonomics* will show you how TRUST (truth, relevance, unselfishness, simplicity, and timing) is the secret to getting the connections you desperately seek."

—Joey Coleman,
Chief Experience Composer at Design Symphony
and author of *Your Personal IPO: Taking Yourself
Public to the World*

Being truly liked as a brand is not about the size of a number. It's about being human—trustworthy and believable. Rohit will draw you in with his engaging storytelling style and his principles of *Likeonomics* will inspire you to rethink how you look at marketing.

—David Alston,
CMO, Salesforce Radian6

Finally, likeability is no longer a black box! Bhargava has unearthed prime forces that will help you make an impact in what matters most to you.

—Scott Belsky,
CEO of Behance,
author of *Making Ideas Happen*

Wow! I loved this book! Rohit Bhargava has written an engaging manifesto for our times that should be required reading for everyone who wants to be a success and make a lasting difference in the world. This is a great follow up to Personality Not Included.

—Garr Reynolds,
author of *Presentation Zen* and *The Naked Presenter*,
and Professor of Management,
Kansai Gaidai University

"*Likeonomics* picks up where Dale Carnegie left off by applying important principles to the modern hyper-socially connected era, in which relationships now transcend online and off with equal importance and regularity."

—Frank Gruber,
CEO and co-founder of Tech Cocktail

"In a world exploding with information and competition, the biggest question facing each of us is how do we know which information to trust? Rohit Bhargava's *Likeonomics* offers a powerful strategy that every professional woman needs to hear—that your ability to build powerful and likeable relationships with others is the ultimate key to identifying the best choice of information."

—Marsha Firestone, PhD
Founder and President, Women Presidents' Organization

likeonomics

The Unexpected Truth Behind Earning Trust, Influencing Behavior, and Inspiring Action

Rohit Bhargava

WILEY

John Wiley & Sons, Inc.

Published by John Wiley & Sons, Inc., Hoboken, New Jersey.
Published simultaneously in Canada.

For general information on our other products and services or for technical support, please contact our
Customer Care Department within the United States at (800) 762-2974, outside the United States at
(317) 572-3993 or fax (317) 572-4002.

Wiley publishes in a variety of print and electronic formats and by print-on-demand. Some material
included with standard print versions of this book may not be included in e-books or in
print-on-demand. If this book refers to media such as a CD or DVD that is not included in the
version you purchased, you may download this material at http://booksupport.wiley.com. For more
information about Wiley products, visit www.wiley.com.

Library of Congress Cataloging-in-Publication Data:
Bhargava, Rohit.
   Likeonomics : the unexpected truth behind earning trust, influencing behavior, and inspiring
action / Rohit Bhargava.
      p. cm.
   Includes index.
   ISBN 978-1-118-13753-6 (cloth); ISBN 978-1-118-22535-6 (ebk); ISBN 978-1-118-23882-0
(ebk); ISBN 978-1-118-26344-0 (ebk)
   1. Economics—Psychological aspects. 2. Marketing—Psychological aspects. 3. Trust. 4. Charisma
(Personality trait) 5. Interpersonal relations. 6. Customer relations. 7. Public relations. I. Title.
   HB74.P8B52 2012
   658.8'12—dc23

                                                                        2012004860

Printed in the United States of America

10 9 8 7 6 5 4 3 2 1

For Anil Dada, who gave me my first chance to
be a marketer and left us far too early.

"The more people trust you, the more they buy from you."

—David Ogilvy

Contents

Warning: Unexpected Honesty. . .

This Book Is *Not* about the Like Button!

This is not a book about Facebook. It is not really about social media, either. If you are looking for a book about either of those topics, *I would highly suggest that you do not buy this book.*

Not many books start off with a declaration of why you shouldn't buy them, but maybe more should. Maybe more businesses should do the same thing. Honesty isn't something that comes easily today. In our society of constant manipulation, everyone from businesses to politicians to the media want us to buy something, believe something, or do something.

The biggest crisis in our world today is one of believability. It makes it tougher to build a successful business, find and keep a job, or convince anyone to do or believe in anything.

This is a book about trust. But it is not another obvious declaration that trust matters. I think you probably already know that. The big idea behind Likeonomics is that you cannot build trust without being likeable. In the 1980s, Japanese businessmen adopted the word *dochakuka* to describe the idea that communities and people could think globally but act locally.

Likeonomics is a word to describe a similar idea. It is a way of looking at the world simultaneously on a large and

> **The most important global currency isn't made of paper anymore—it's made of relationships.**

small scale. Whether you are launching your own business, or trying to land a job, or working to win an election—the principles are the same.

As you'll see in *Likeonomics*, the idea of likeability goes far beyond getting people to like you on a superficial level. It is not just about being nice. Instead, we will look at how people and organizations lose trust, how they can get it back, and what it really takes to be more believable.

My first step in building a relationship with you is to make sure you're buying this book because you know what you'll get out of it. My second is to try and offer a nonobvious and entertaining roadmap for how to be more believable in an irrational and information overloaded world. So let's get started.

Prologue:
How a Lard Salesman, an NFL Agent, and a YouTube Star Explain Likeonomics

Just over 10 years ago, I was part of a pitch that I knew we would win. I was leading of one of the hottest and fastest growing digital production teams in Australia. We had built a glowing reputation in our market, won tons of creative awards, and boasted a long list of top-notch references.

More importantly, our creative concept and strategy for the potential client we were about to meet was perfect, and we knew it. We had such an original approach, in fact, that we knew none of our competitors would even come close.

By the pitch day, our team had rehearsed for two days straight and we were supremely confident. It showed. The meeting went almost perfectly. Everyone knew their part, and the client asked the right questions. As we walked out, we allowed ourselves to enjoy a momentary feeling of triumph.

We were ready to take a victory call the next day and accept the client's business. It was just a matter of time. Like clockwork, we got the call the very next day, as expected. Only the outcome wasn't what we expected. We had lost.

In the weeks afterward, our team went back over every step. What did we get wrong? How could we have lost? We simply couldn't understand. It was one of those rare situations where if we had the chance to go in and pitch again, we wouldn't have done anything differently. We longed to know the amazing idea that we lost against. Unfortunately, we never got a good answer. It was the first time in my career when I learned the frustrating lesson that sometimes you lose and never really get to know why.

A year later, I was at an industry conference and happened to see that same client we had pitched to. I asked her how they were doing, and exchanged some polite conversation. With nothing to lose, I then asked her the question really on my mind: *Why didn't we win?* She looked at me and told me something I have never forgotten: "You guys had great ideas and they did, too," she admitted. "Honestly, we chose them because we just liked their team better. We *wanted* to work with them."

It didn't seem fair. It still doesn't—but now I understand. Since that time, I have had countless pieces of business won or lost over this single metric of team chemistry, but relatively few clients with the personal insight and ability to understand or admit how critical this piece was to their decision.

The fact is, the significance of this goes far beyond just the world of business.

People trust and choose to believe people they like.

We all choose our friends and teammates for everything from work to hobbies based on likeability. Relationships, not logic, power almost all of our decisions. **In order to be more believable and more trusted—you need to be more likeable.** That is the simple idea behind this book.

To see why this idea matters so much, let's begin the journey by going backward in history to 1912 and a dusty classroom in Harlem, New York, where one of the most enduring philosophies of modern business was first born—even though no one there that night knew it.

The Lard Salesman

It was 6 p.m. in a dimly lit classroom at the YMCA Harlem Evening School in early 1912, and the instructor was nervous. His topic that night was public speaking, and even though more than half the seats were empty, his heart still raced. At 24 years old, he had already dropped out of college and failed as a young actor. His only modest success in his short career so far had been rising to become the number one salesman of "the highest quality tins of lard" (yes, lard) in western South Dakota.

That night he had walked to the classroom from his small, roach-filled apartment in a part of New York City that easily lived up to its nickname of "Hell's Kitchen." He certainly didn't look too well, as his biographers would later write: "You could tell he had come upon hard times . . . [as] though one warm bowl of soup might have been enough to restore an appearance of health."

Standing there in his ill-fitting gray suit and wire-rimmed glasses, he was struck by a sudden sense of panic.

What was he doing here?

Why would anyone want to listen to him?

His mind went blank.

By any account, he was an unlikely character to teach anything, much less public speaking. His voice was often described as possessing a slow, rambling Midwestern twang. He wasn't a politician, or a famous athlete, or even a radio personality. He was the poor son of a pig farmer in Missouri who desperately wanted more than anything else to avoid becoming a farmer like his father.

If he was going to become famous, it certainly wouldn't be from his chosen topic for that night either. In the early 1900s, public speaking was not as popular a professional skill as it has become today. Despite his ambition, the obscurity of his topic meant that he had already been turned down by both Columbia and NYU for his lecture. In desperation he had made a deal with the director of the YMCA to deliver his course by agreeing to forego the customary night teacher salary of $2 per course. Instead, he would share in the profit—with the unspoken understanding that there probably wouldn't be any. Finally, after all that work, his first class was happening and he could feel his big chance fading away before it had even begun.

In his moment of panic that night, a sudden burst of inspiration hit him. He asked a man in the back row of the classroom to stand up and talk about himself and his life. Then he asked another student to do the same. And then another. That simple format got people talking because they were each listening to personal stories that brought them together.

In this moment, he would learn an important insight that would shape his career from then on. There is nothing people care about more than being able to build better relationships with the others around them. This was, in fact, a skill that they would even be willing to pay to learn.

There was a phrase for this new skill . . . *human relations*. It started to be used to describe the ability to get along with and influence other people. So that year, building on his original insight, he formally named his new and improved course on human relations after himself: *The Dale Carnegie Course in Public Speaking and Human Relations.*

He would go on to fanatically refine and improve the course for the next 24 years. In one class he would use improvisational acting techniques; in another he would have participants do one-on-one exercises. The course spread to thousands of students and turned Carnegie into something of a business celebrity. He was filling large auditoriums with willing students, but it was in 1936 (almost a quarter of a century after starting his course) that he would achieve his biggest claim to fame.

That year a persistent editor at Simon & Schuster finally convinced Carnegie to write a book based on his course. The title would be easy: *How to Win Friends and Influence People.* The book was an instant best seller. Over the next decade, the book became the second bestselling book of its time, after the Bible.

Meanwhile, Carnegie's course grew into a full training Institute. In 2011, his Institute celebrated the seventy-fifth anniversary of the book's first printing. In that time, the book has been translated into over 60 languages and sold more than 16 million copies worldwide.

Today, everyone from business executives to political leaders from around the world have studied the principles and are using them to transform the way they relate to other people. More than 2,700 professional trainers offer Dale Carnegie's course in 80 countries and 27 languages. The Institute has trained over 7 million graduates across the world.

The NFL Agent

In law school, you don't spend too much time learning how to win friends. Chitta Mallik, however, never wanted to be an ordinary lawyer.

His real passion was football, but sports law was about the closest he expected to get. After graduating law school, he accepted a job at Latham & Watkins, one of the largest and most respected firms in the United States.

In October of 2004, after realizing that he had billed 434 hours that month (an average of 14 hours a day, every day, including weekends!), he decided it was time for a change. A lifelong sports fan, he knew that he wanted a career in sports. And despite working in sports law, Mallik realized what he really wanted to do was become an NFL agent. Unfortunately, it was an almost impossible field to break into.

Around the same time, a former standout NFL player named Tony Paige had been growing his own services as a highly successful NFL Agent. Paige had been a starting fullback in the NFL for nine seasons, an extraordinarily long career in a dangerous sport where the average career lasts only about three years. He got his accidental start as an agent shortly after he retired by agreeing to help a desperate former teammate renegotiate his contract. He did more in a week than the player's agent had done for him in years. As anyone inside the NFL knows, there are generally two types of players: those that get attention from their agents and those that don't. Agents are notorious for following the money, focusing their time and attention on their most highly paid clients—and shortchanging the rest. Most of them have little idea of what it takes to succeed in the NFL. Of the over 600 agents officially licensed by the NFL Player's Association to represent players, less than 15 are former players themselves.

So Paige had a natural advantage, but he also started in the business with a unique philosophy. While most agents cared about the player, he also tried to care about the person. This meant he would become a part of his player's lives. He would advise them on everything from buying a house to donating their time to charities. He was a genuinely good guy in a job where that was sadly uncommon.

In the spring of 2008, Mallik met Paige for the first time through a personal connection. Within 5 minutes, it was clear that the two men shared the same business philosophy and morals. Paige quickly convinced Mallik to join forces and help him run the Football Division at Perennial Sports and Entertainment, a full-service sports agency. Later that year, one of the first players they signed together was a 6-foot-2, 315-pound offensive lineman named Cecil Newton Jr. Newton had played college football at Tennessee State University and entered the NFL draft in 2009. Unfortunately, he wasn't selected, but Paige and Mallik worked hard to find him a home in the NFL. They paid for his training, and reminded him that as long as he was in the building, he had a chance. Newton finally landed a rookie contract with the Jacksonville Jaguars. That year, he made it onto the field and actually played. The NFL is full of small victories like Newton's but the story doesn't end there.

Two years later, Cecil's younger brother Cameron was about to enter the NFL draft. Cameron, or "Cam," Newton had been a star quarterback who had won the Heisman Trophy (the highest individual award offered to college football athletes) and led his Auburn Tigers college team to the BCS National Championship. For the 2011 draft, he was anticipated to be among the first 10 players picked overall. As a result, he had his pick of an NFL agent, and 12 agencies were all courting him.

But Cecil's father had promised Mallik and Paige they would have a chance to meet with Cam—and he kept his promise. They met with him in January of 2011, amidst 11 other agencies desperately selling their own services. Yet, instead of talking to him about his future as a player, they talked about his future as a man.

They asked him what he wanted to be known for. They talked about what life after football would be like. And they talked about his brother. At the end of the first round of meetings, Cam and his father called back Perennial Sports. In January of 2011, Newton announced that he had selected Paige and Mallik along with Bus Cook, another agent.

It was like a real-life moment from the film *Jerry Maguire* where the agent wins the client based on his principles.

Six months later, Cam Newton was drafted by the Carolina Panthers with the number-one overall pick in the 2011 NFL draft, and signed to a four-year, $22 million contract. In his first game ever, he became the first rookie to throw for 400 yards in his regular NFL-season opening game. Through the rest of his first season, he would go on to break more than a dozen other rookie quarterback records.

For Paige, Mallik, and Perennial Sports, landing the #1 overall pick in the NFL draft was a defining moment. The following year, they were two of the hottest agents in the league and went on to have their most successful draft class ever.

The YouTube Star

For Ana Gomes Ferreira, the first YouTube video was just for fun. It was January of 2007 and she was sitting on her bed with a guitar in her lap. With a friend holding the video camera, she recorded her own version of Sheryl Crow's "Strong Enough to Be My Man" and uploaded it under her stage name, "Ana Free." As song goes on, the camera zooms in and out randomly. The audio is muffled and you can tell that she isn't entirely comfortable in front of the camera.

You would never, at any point during that video, have mistaken Ana Free for anything more than a girl just having fun. It would be a nice story if she was discovered by an enterprising music executive, but that's not how her future would go. Her first video didn't get a million views. She was never meant to become another viral one-hit wonder—but that was perfectly fine for Ana.

As a child in Portugal, Ana didn't grow up wanting to be a singer. She went to an international school, studied hard, spoke five languages, and studied international trade and game theory while majoring in economics at the University of Kent in the United Kingdom. She had the sort of background that would usually have led a smart, young enterprising woman toward a career at a big institution like the World Bank or IMF.

All of which makes what would happen over the next five years even more extraordinary.

Every day, dozens of budding musicians look to the Internet as a place to get discovered and perhaps duplicate the phenomenon of Justin Bieber—by launching themselves and their music careers. Almost no one succeeds.

Ana, however, had one important thing going for her—she didn't start uploading her videos in order to be famous. She started by performing songs that she loved and then sharing them honestly with her audience. And unlike so many other musicians, she didn't avoid playing cover songs or gaining popularity by playing songs that people recognized.

Despite having written hundreds of her own original songs, every few weeks she would record a video of a new cover song that people recognized. Each song featured her sitting on a bed or a couch playing her acoustic guitar and singing directly to the camera. She has a great voice and slowly gets more and more comfortable in front of the camera. The audio improves. She buys a tripod. You can actually see her getting better from video to video. Yet the thing that sets every one of her videos apart is that they are all a surprisingly intimate musical experience.

When she sings and looks directly at the camera, it *feels* like she is singing directly to you. She shares outtakes where she breaks guitar strings and forgets lyrics. And her audience has grown because she is so genuinely passionate about the songs she sings, even when those songs have been written by someone else. As one music critic wrote, "The thing about Ana Free is her voice . . . [it] has a rawness that seems to reach into my chest and pluck on my heart like a guitar string. Not too high, more of a husky tenor."[1] Before long, each of her songs started routinely getting thousands and then tens of thousands of views.

By early 2012, Ana had posted over 125 songs onto her YouTube channel—and almost every one had more than 10,000 views. More than a dozen have over 100,000 views. Several of her songs racked up more than 2 million views each, and her channel on YouTube has passed 31 million views overall and more than 80,000 subscribers. In June of 2010, her cover performance of Shakira's World Cup 2010 theme song "Waka Waka" was so popular that it inspired Shakira's production team to invite Ana Free to be an opening act for a Shakira concert in South America.

She has played at international music festivals around the world, and in 2008, her independently released debut single "In My Place" shot to the number-one spot on the Portuguese music charts. Three years later, she released her first EP, called *Radian*, and she will soon be releasing her first full-length album in 2012 (thanks to a highly successful social media–led fundraising effort from engaged fans).

Perhaps the greatest symbol of her ever-growing influence comes from looking back at YouTube itself. In 2011, a group of four young female fans of Ana Free launched their very own group who go to her concerts and record their own videos as a tribute to her influence. Their "anafreecrew" YouTube channel has already generated more than 25,000 views.

The Big Question

What do a Portuguese singer who launched her career on YouTube, a reformed lawyer who became a successful sports agent, and the author of the world's most popular personal development book have in common?

Ana Free had the ability to connect personally with her audience in a deep and meaningful way by authentically sharing her personality and singing songs that people already knew and loved.

Chitta Mallik achieved the greatest goal of a NFL sports agent (getting a client who goes number one in the draft) by building a personal relationship with his client's family and becoming a trusted expert.

Dale Carnegie's success was based on the relationships he was able to cultivate with others, and his ability to teach people to learn the same skill—what he called human relations.

Each of these stories, in its own way, is about the power of relationships. Humans are social creatures. We choose to build relationships and do business with people we know and like. In a world of crowded media, with lots of organizations, politicians, and people competing for our attention, the key to success is your ability to earn trust. Trusted businesses are more profitable. Trusted people are more influential and successful. Trusted ideas are more likely to inspire belief. And being more believable is the toughest challenge for anyone today, which leads to the question at the heart of *Likeonomics* (see box) . . .

> **How can any person, organization, or idea become more trusted and more believable?**

The rest of this book will be dedicated to answering that question.

Why Likeonomics Matters

At first glance, the idea behind Likeonomics might seem like an oversimplified way of looking at the world. After all, don't real technical skills or talent matter more than likeability? When it comes to business, can't likeability be faked by people who just want to take our money and sell us stuff? And perhaps the most common challenge against likeability: Isn't making a great product or offering a great service more important than likeability on any level?

In *Likeonomics*, I'll tackle each of these objections. We will look at examples of everything from getting movies made in Hollywood to winning contracts to clean toilets. The people featured in *Likeonomics* come from around the world and range from some of the world's most recognizable CEOs to up and coming creators. What they all have in common is a shared understanding of how our world works.

It is a world where the most trusted people and organizations always win. It doesn't matter if you are looking for your next job, or trying to turn your own business into a success, or just build better relationships in your local community. This book is about how to earn and keep trust—and be more believable.

To see how, let's start with what might be one of the most powerful and global examples of the power of likeability and how it helped to change the fortunes of an entire nation.

Introduction: Likeability, Rogue Economists, and the Lovable Fool

If you talk to a man in a language he understands, that goes to his head. If you talk to him in his language, that goes to his heart.

—Nelson Mandela

The first time I experienced the powerful influence of Nelson Mandela was from the front seat of a taxi cab riding down the streets of Jo'burg (as the locals call Johannesburg). Mandela's picture was on billboards along the highway to the city even though he was no longer president of South Africa, and my driver was speaking about his influence and how he had inspired the nation. That story started nearly 20 years ago.

In 1993, tens of thousands of Afrikaners (white South Africans) were preparing for war. Three years earlier, a man named Nelson Mandela had been released after 27 years in prison. He was no hero to this group. They saw him as the founder of a terrorist organization who threatened their way of life and belonged in jail. They were ready to fight.

As reporter and biographer John Carlin wrote, that was the moment where Mandela began "the most unlikely exercise in political seduction ever undertaken."[1] He invited the Afrikaners leaders over for tea and listened to their concerns. Then, he persuaded them to abandon their guns and violence. The battle never happened.

A year later, he was sworn in as president of South Africa and vowed to make reconciling the racial tension between whites and blacks his number-one priority. Somehow he had to overcome decades of hate and convince people ready to die for their causes to see one another as brothers.

In one of his first acts as president, Mandela invited Francois Pienaar, the captain of the South Africa national rugby team (Springboks), to have tea with him. That afternoon he struck an alliance, asking Pienaar to help him turn rugby into a force for uniting all South Africans.

During the Rugby World Cup in 1995, Pienaars led the mostly white players of the Springbok team in singing an old song of black resistance, which was now the new national anthem, "Nkosi Sikelele Afrika" ("God Bless Africa"). It was a powerful demonstration that the players believed in having a united South Africa. Inspired, the team fought the odds and made it to the finals against Australia.

On June 24, 1995, minutes before the final match would start, Mandela went on the field in the middle of the stadium wearing his Springbok green shirt to wish Pienaar and the team good luck. The crowd, made up of mostly white South Africans, was stunned. For many years, that green shirt had been seen as a symbol of only white South Africa. For a black man to wear it was unheard of.

The crowd erupted in cheers of "Nel-son, Nel-son" and everyone across South Africa celebrated. Mandela would go on to lead the racial reconciliation both during his presidency, and then after as an ambassador to the world for South Africa. In 2004, the country was awarded the world's largest stage to host the 2010 FIFA World Cup. It is now seen as a likely future Olympic destination, as well.

This story of South Africa's triumph was chronicled by Carlin in his book *Playing the Enemy: Nelson Mandela and the Game That Made a Nation*. It was so powerful, it also inspired the Academy Award–winning film *Invictus* by director Clint Eastwood.

Why People Believe in Likeability (and Why They Don't)

The fate of South Africa is linked to the story of one man's personal charm and likeability. This may seem like an extreme example. After all, not many people have the gift that Mandela has. Yet, his experience does explain the very fundamental role that likeability can take in inspiring belief and changing our world around us. People didn't follow Mandela because of the ideas; they followed because of *him*. When he invited you over for tea and listened to your concerns, and then spoke, you couldn't help trusting his vision.

But likeability itself can be a difficult idea to believe in, because it feels *soft*. In doing the research and writing for this book over the past year, I have had hundreds of conversations with people about the concept of likeability. When I started conducting interviews, I assumed that almost everyone would be a skeptic.

What I learned rapidly was that most people actually fall into two different groups. Both can be critical about the idea of likeability and its role in success, but for different reasons. Here are their paraphrased arguments:

Reaction #1: "That's so obvious."

Here's what "Obvious Guy" says:

> Everyone knows that likeability and the power of networking will get you everything from your new job to the next contract. I once won a new project just because I play hockey with the procurement manager for a big firm and they needed a contractor quickly. We won the job without an RFP. Anyone in sales knows that no one will buy from you if they don't like you.

Reaction #2: "That's not true—the product matters more."

Here's what "Features Guy" says:

> Sure, I enjoy being around likeable people—but at the end of the day people will only buy something or believe an idea if it really has merit. I'm not going to buy a crap product just because I like you, and I'm not going to believe an idea just because I find the person delivering it to be more likeable.

I understand both of these guys. In fact, at various times in the writing process for this book, I have *been* both of these guys. In a sense, it is why I spent a significant part of my research time looking at all the reasons why likeability wasn't really that important. I studied examples of unlikeable leaders and brands that still succeeded on some level despite being unlikeable. I read books about the impact of luck and the importance of making great products that market themselves. I dug backward through history, looking at whether the importance of likeability was different during the Great Depression or the golden age of Sweden.

> **What I learned is that success has much less to do with *what* we create and much more to do with *who* believes in it.**

This is not about creating an awful product and trying to use likeability to sell it. It is also not about trying to fake likeability to support some sort of sinister ulterior motive. I will speak about how to handle both of these situations later in the book.

Instead, my aim is to look at the intersection of likeability and the global economy and offer a vision of how any one of us can build the kinds of relationships that lead to all kinds of personal success—from launching a business to getting a new job.

The Nonboring Economics of Likeonomics

The unlikeliest place to start a discussion about the impact of likeability on the economy would be in the field of economics itself. One of the first things I did in my research, in fact, was to look at what leading economists might have already published about the main idea of this book. An economist, as writer Laurence J. Peter once wrote, "is an expert who will know tomorrow why the things he predicted yesterday didn't happen today."

Luckily, this is not really an economics book and Likeonomics is not an economic theory in a strict sense. Rather, it is an attempt to describe the world that we live in today and what people and business professionals alike need to do in order to survive and thrive in it. Unlike many traditional economists, I tend to avoid academic thinking and language, preferring instead to think about the world in terms of human interactions rather than numbers in a spreadsheet. It turns out these are not the opposing factors that they once were, as the world of economics learned the day the surprising results of the voting for the winners of the 2002 Nobel Prize for Economic Sciences were announced.

The Psychology of Likeonomics

Dr. Daniel Kahneman was once described by Harvard psychologist Daniel Gilbert as "the most distinguished living psychologist in the world, bar none." Along with partner Amos Tversky, his lifetime of work in applying psychological principles of how people behave to economic theory essentially led directly to what we today call the field of behavioral economics. When they were awarded the Nobel Prize in 2002, the awarding committee credited Kahneman for "for having integrated insights from psychological research into economic science, especially concerning human judgment and decision-making under uncertainty."

The idea that people are not logical robots, but rather that they respond to incentives and are led by emotions is still a relatively recent idea.

For a field once called the "dismal science" by the Victorian historian Thomas Carlyle in the nineteenth century, one of its strongest mainstream boosts for the importance of economics would come in 2005 with the publication of *Freakonomics*, which also inspired the title for this book.

The authors of *Freakonomics* like to use the description "rogue economist" to describe their take on the world. Part economics and part social psychology, they merged these worlds together successfully in a groundbreaking book that explains why we behave the way we do, why seemingly unrelated phenomena from across the world may be linked, and how our understanding of what motivates our behaviors may not be as simple and rational as we like to think.

Since *Freakonomics*, this theme of the irrationality of behavior is one that has become extremely popular in multiple best-selling books.

Just because we respond to emotional appeals and tend to act in human ways, however, doesn't necessarily prove that likeability is all that important. After all,

> **Each book reaches a related conclusion—that people act in emotional, human, and unexpected ways, and respond to incentives. We are not logical robots.**

there seem to be plenty of examples of leaders who are successful despite being frequently described as unlikeable. Like Steve Jobs, for instance.

The Jobs Paradox

The late Steve Jobs was clearly visionary and had a brilliant mind, but was also often described as egomaniacal and hard to work with. A *Boston Globe* review of the biography of Jobs by veteran journalist Walter Isaacson, released just a few weeks after Jobs's death begins with this pronouncement about him: "Life often reduced Steve Jobs to tears. But he rarely suffered alone. The cofounder of Apple, Inc., spread his unhappiness like a virus, abusing his friends, neglecting his family, insulting and reviling his colleagues. And almost to a person, they loved Jobs to the end."[2]

> **This is what we might call the Jobs Paradox—that some people can seem to be completely unlikeable, and yet succeed and inspire those close to them regardless.**

And Jobs was hardly the only unlikeable leader in Silicon Valley, either.

Larry Ellison, the founder of Oracle, has developed a reputation for being an unlikeable character, as well. He has made fun of rivals on stage at the Oracle annual OpenWorld conference and attacked former Sun rival and CEO Jonathan Schwartz for "spending too much time on his blog." When asked about Bill Gates, he famously said, "Referring to Gates as the smartest man in America isn't right. Wealth isn't the same thing as intelligence."

When Bloomberg television decided to do a feature on Ellison for their *Game Changers* series, Oracle co-founder Bruce Scott was interviewed and shared, "I remember [Ellison] very distinctly telling me one time: Bruce, we can't be successful unless we lie to customers. All the things that you would read in books of somebody being a leader, he wasn't."

When asked about his personal philosophy, Ellison once said: "I don't believe in being nice to my enemies. My enemies are trying to deprive me of the success that led to my happiness. I want to beat my enemies, and it's hard to be nice to them at the same time."[3]

There are probably dozens of other examples of this paradox. So what does it mean? Are the business clichés like "nice guys finish last" or "nice girls don't get the corner office" actually right? And if likeability matters so much, how can we explain the success of these two men who seemed to make arrogance and competition their priorities? The answer comes down to understanding the difference between likeability and being nice because of the human need to be liked.

Do We Need to Be Liked?

People who care too much about being liked are often described as weak or insecure. As a result, few people and even fewer business leaders are ready to admit that they care about it or even factor likeability into any of their everyday decisions. So if likeability is such a hard quality to admit to caring about, why is the need to be liked such a powerful motivational force? If anyone has the answer, it is Dr. Roger Corvin, a clinical psychologist practicing in Montreal who has spent his career trying to help patients with a variety of mental or emotional issues.

His average afternoon might include seeing a depressed teen, an executive with anxiety, and a mother with post-traumatic stress disorder (PTSD). Despite the variety of genders, life situations, ages, and ethnicities, Dr. Corvin started to realize that there was a common trait among all the people who came to see him: They all had a need to be liked by other people.

In his book, *The Need to Be Liked*, he describes this as a *fundamental human need* in psychological terms because:

1. The brain and body are designed to acquire it.
2. Not fulfilling the need has negative effects on the person.

The primary function of this need, he argues, is to "ensure that we form relationships with other people." There is a clear evolutionary reason why this would have mattered for our ancestors: Those who were able to form relationships and work together were more likely to survive.

So what about the curious cases of Jobs and Ellison? Were they simply immune to this need to be liked and therefore able to behave more harshly?

The answer to the Jobs Paradox lies in Dr. Colvin's point about the many qualities of likeability. Likeability is about being able to personally connect with people on a different level. Jobs, despite his well-known ego and arrogance, had a talent for telling the truth, which people loved and respected.

A few months before Jobs passed away, Nike CEO Mark Parker was asked by an interviewer about the best piece of advice he had ever been given. He recalled calling Jobs shortly after becoming CEO and asking him for any advice. "Well, just one thing," said Jobs. "Nike makes some of the best products in the world. Products that you lust after. But you also make a lot of crap. Just get rid of the crappy stuff and focus on the good stuff."

He wasn't joking. It was that type of honesty and clarity of vision that attracted people to Jobs. It made him likeable, in his own way. It also illustrates an important point of difference.

Being likeable is not the same thing as being nice.

Ellison also seemed to have a different standard for how he would behave depending on who he was dealing with. In an interview for *Softwar*, Ellison noted that "Being insensitive, rude or mean to someone close to you, or a perfect stranger for that matter, is self-destructive and self-degrading behavior. You'll think less of yourself for doing it."

Understanding that likeability doesn't mean the same thing to everyone may seem like a confusing contradiction. As we will soon see, however, likeability is enough to compensate for some very real human failings. In Jobs' case, it may be extreme arrogance. In other cases, as two behavior and decision sciences professors learned, it may even be a lack of competence.

The Hidden Appeal of the Likeable Fool

In 2005, Tiziana Casciaro, a Harvard Business School professor, and Miguel Sousa Lobo, a professor of decision sciences at Duke University, decided to find out just how important likeability was in a business context. Together, they conducted a series of surveys at four organizations: a Silicon Valley tech company, a division of an IT corporation, a U.S.

university, and the Spanish country office of a global luxury goods corporation. Combining this with results from surveys filled out by a large group of MBA students, they ultimately collected and studied data from over 10,000 work relationships.

Everyone they spoke to was plotted against two characteristics based on how they answered questions and how their peers rated them: their likeability and their competence. They then asked participants to imagine they had a job to do at work. Which of their colleagues would they choose to work with? On one level, the results were completely predictable.

Everyone wanted to work with the highly likeable and highly competent individuals (who the study dubbed the "Lovable Star"), and no one wanted to work with the low competence and low likeability individuals (the "Incompetent Jerk"). The unexpected results came when looking at the other two categories.

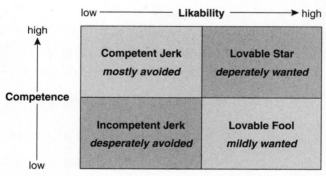

The study demonstrated that when faced with a choice between a more likeable person who workers had a stronger personal relationship with, or someone who had better job performance, but was less likeable—most people chose to work with the "Lovable Fool" (low competence, high likeability) rather than the "Competent Jerk" (high competence, low likeability).

The conclusion of the study was clear: "When faced with a choice between a 'competent jerk' and a 'lovable fool' as a work partner, people usually opt for likeability over ability." This is not an isolated finding, either. Consider these results from research conducted around the world over the past few decades:

- In a communications study from 2003, researchers at the University of Michigan uncovered that "friendly and positive employees are more productive."
- A 1984 study by the University of California showed that doctors unconsciously spend more time and offer better quality care to patients they like.
- In his book *Making Your Case: The Art of Persuading Judges*, U.S. Supreme Court Justice Antonin Scalia wrote of the importance of being likeable and how it leads to trust. "Some people," he noted, "are inherently likeable. If you're not, work on it."
- A study in 2001 from Columbia University found that the more popular and likeable workers were seen as trustworthy, motivated, decisive, and hard-working, and as such were recommended for fast-track promotions and pay raises.

Across the business world and beyond, likeability has a fundamental power to help us build trust in our interactions with others.

Inside Part I: The Crisis and the Solution

Of course, likeability on some level has always mattered, so why write this book *now*—and why does it matter so much to understanding our world, behavior, and global economy?

Part I of the book will tackle these important questions by looking at the very real believability crisis that we are in, how we got here, and why the idea behind Likeonomics offers a vision for where we need to go next.

In **Chapter 1: Inside the Modern Believability Crisis**, we look backward at the rise of propaganda and how trust in business and institutions has reached an all-time low. You will read how an unexpected public relations campaign for an oil tycoon in the early 1900s jump-started our "modern believability crisis," and why marketing is often the source of all manipulation. Moving quickly through the past hundred years, we will see how this growth in manipulation on every level has created an unprecedented challenge for each of us (and the organizations we work with) to inspire or motivate people to do or believe in anything.

Moving to **Chapter 2: Navigating the Likeability Gap**, the concept of the "likeability gap" will help to explain the nature of how we decide and why we choose to work with and help people and organizations that we like. Through the story of the rise of Rwanda and the real reason why so many million-dollar deals start on the golf course, this chapter will look at why relationships matter so much and how being more likeable is the key to building trust.

Finally, in **Chapter 3: The ROI of Likeability**, we will look at what the real business and personal value is behind the concept of Likeonomics. This chapter will move from analyzing decades of research into education reform, to the story of why ROI was originally invented (it's not what you think). Ultimately, we will tackle several flawed assumptions about measurement and look at some new ideas for how to really measure success and why it is *not* about creating a better spreadsheet.

Inside Part II: The Principles

After the focus of Part I on demonstrating all the ways that Likeonomics explains the world we live in today, Part II will go deeper to offer a practical and useful look at why people trust some organizations or people and not others—and how you can be more trusted and more believable in anything you do.

In looking at all the research about how people and organizations become more believable, as well as the impact that social media has had on how we interact with one another and companies, I wanted to uncover some key principles for what really matters when it comes to being more believable. My aim was to find these principles and then create some sort of acronym to describe them. As readers of my blog already know, using acronyms is a method I often use to make new ideas more memorable.

So one day more than a year ago, I gathered all of my research together and started to define what I thought were the most important principles. The starting point was research that had addressed a similar challenge:

1. **The Likeability Factor**—I looked at Tim Sanders' award-winning work in *The Likeability Factor*, about how to be more likeable as a person. His four "elements of likeability" came down to friendliness, relevance, empathy, and realness. In his mind, these were in "green light order," which meant you had to be friendly before you could be relevant, and so on.

2. **The Netherlands Study**—Twenty years ago, the Advertising Research Foundation set their research agenda for 1991 and proposed that studying the impact of likeability on advertising research should be a key topic. That year, several research studies on the topic were conducted and three authors in the Netherlands decided to launch a 10-year study on the effects of advertising likeability. Their results, published in 2006, proposed that there were four components to advertising likeability: entertainment, relevance, clearness, and pleasantness.

As I sat down one afternoon in February to put some of the research down on paper, five core principles seemed to leap out from all the work I had done. In fact, it was so clear that I assumed they must be wrong or too simple. Since that afternoon in February, I revisited my initial acronym almost every week for months with the intention of changing it.

I did more research, consumed more reports, and read more books. I spoke with colleagues and clients to try and poke holes in the idea. I even presented the acronym during a speech in Miami to get a public reaction and have others criticize it. It still worked.

What was even better, the principles I had landed on spelled a powerful acronym that would fit perfectly into the main point I wanted to make in the book:

TRUST = **T**RUTH + **R**ELEVANCE + **U**NSELFISHNESS
+ **S**IMPLICITY + **T**IMING

So in Part II of the book, we will dig into each of these five principles of Likeonomics to look at why they matter, and offer a practical guidebook on how you can use them.

Principle 1: Truth—There is no more important quality than the real truth, and we live in a time where people are more able to demand it than ever. This is not, however, the same thing as honesty. In this chapter, we will learn from the meteoric rise of the most famous talk show host in history, to the story of a struggling brand that took an unheard of risk in telling the truth about why they would always fail to be number one in their industry.

Principle 2: Relevance—The challenge to be relevant requires that you center yourself on the world that someone else already cares about. Using global stories of how to shake hands in Kazakhstan and why Canada's favorite storyteller became so beloved, this chapter will define exactly what makes something or someone powerfully relevant, and how you can do it for yourself or your business.

Principle 3: Unselfishness—If there is one principle that seems dramatically hard to consistently do, it is behaving in an unselfish way. Combining the story of how a small yet powerful networking group is taking their region by storm and what one of the largest global studies of unselfish corporate behavior has proven about the role of idealism in branding, this section will prove that being unselfish pays off in many ways, and is a necessity for success in our new global economy.

Principle 4: Simplicity—Of all the principles, this one has near universal agreement from leading thinkers in the world about its importance. Simplicity is the force that has powered the Apple brand to success and also driven politicians to win elections and world-changing social movements to build a following. In this chapter, we will not only learn how much simplicity can help to achieve, but also some new and completely different methods for simplifying everything from messaging to how you spend your time.

Principle 5: Timing—Some of the greatest ideas in human history have succeeded or failed based entirely on timing. More than just suggesting that good timing matters, we will look at the examples of how people are always at the heart of timing, and understanding when to push your idea is the crucial X-factor that can help ensure success.

Inside Part III: The StoryBook (Likeonomics in Action)

If you are the sort of reader who likes to skip the theory and go straight to the stories and case studies that bring each idea to life, you will appreciate this section.

In addition to the dozens of stories I share throughout this book, this final section spotlights a collection of examples of the principles behind Likeonomics at work. It includes everything from the little known story of what might be the happiest country on Earth, to the website that has turned the world of education upside down.

Stories are what inspire each of us, but they also have to be relevant (remember, that's one of the principles!). So each story will also be indexed by industry so you can browse them to identify the ones that feel closest to your own personal situation.

In addition, this StoryBook will be a living part of Likeonomics online, with new stories getting consistently added to the website. You can always visit **www.likeonomics.com/storybook** to read additional stories, and even add your own story in the online community.

Author's Note: Why I Don't Write about Synergy and Paradigm Shifts

In case you haven't read *Personality Not Included* (my first book), you have probably already noticed that I don't use an "academic" style of writing. Technically, I am a professor, since I teach marketing at Georgetown University, but I also speak around the world on the necessity of being approachable and creating more human businesses, which often starts with language.

In my process of writing *Likeonomics*, there were a few guiding principles I used to remind me of what kind of book I wanted to write. Here are a few of them:

1. **Write like a person, not a professor.** As a writer, I have always been heavily influenced by screenwriting, which means I don't really use too much marketing jargon, opting instead for a more conversational tone. Thanks to a master's degree in English Literature and a BA in Irish Poetry (yes, seriously) and Marketing, I have written and read plenty of academic prose. Personally, I find those kinds of books too stuffy. I'd rather learn from a book that shares ideas and lessons more conversationally, so that's the type of book I aim to write.

2. **Offer real, practical, and useful ideas.** Given that I spend all day as a marketing consultant, leading brand strategy for some of

the biggest brands in the world (in my full-time job at Ogilvy communications agency)—as well as write for one of the largest small business–focused blogs in the world (the American Express Open Forum)—I'm very focused on real and practical ideas for businesses of all sizes.

3. **There is no one perfect industry, country, or brand.** I have gone door to door selling my own startup, as well as led marketing strategy meetings with dozens of participants and millions of dollars at stake. Unlike many vertically focused and process-obsessed marketing consultants, I see many sides of the business story. I know that one method doesn't describe everyone. In this book, I feature big and small brands, global brands, and stories from outside America and dozens of industries—so I can guarantee you will find examples that apply to your situation. If you don't, e-mail me at likeonomics@ gmail.com and I promise to send you one personally.

4. **Business theory can be boring; stories usually aren't.** I have read hundreds of business books (by choice!). Most have good ideas and are written by very smart people. But they are not usually page turners. You understand the big idea, but you have to wade through some pretty boring stuff to get there. My ultimate aim with *Likeonomics* is to be entertaining *and* useful. I often describe it as nonboring and nonobvious. In my experience, there are very few business books that can do both these things.

So now that you have a sense of my philosophy, let's get started with a slightly reworded line that authors have used to begin their tales for centuries:

Once upon a time, there was a crisis . . .

PART I

The Crisis and
the Solution

Inside the Modern Believability Crisis

How Rockefeller's Dimes, War Propaganda, and the Marlboro Man Ruined the World

We are governed, our minds molded, our tastes formed, our ideas suggested, largely by men we have never heard of. Those who manipulate this unseen mechanism of society constitute an invisible government which is the true ruling power of our country.
— Edward Bernays, in *Propaganda*, 1928

About a hundred years ago, one of the world's richest men had a public relations (PR) problem. His name was John D. Rockefeller, and in 1914, he was dealing with a crisis that most of American history has since forgotten.

A decade earlier Rockefeller had purchased the Colorado Fuel and Iron Corporation (CF&I). In the span of those 10 years, CF&I had quickly come to dominate the growing coal mining industry in

Colorado. With 27 dirty and mostly lawless mining camps in Southern Colorado, they had a virtual dictatorship over the many immigrants who worked in the mines. Thanks to the financial success of mining, the company also enjoyed a controlling political influence across the state of Colorado.

Unfortunately, that money never really made it to the miners' pockets, and mining was a hard life. For years the miners suffered under brutal and dangerous working conditions with a lack of basic rights. Finally, the miners decided to create their own organization, United Mine Workers, to negotiate with their corporate masters for better living conditions and (hopefully) higher pay. In 1913, their early negotiations failed. CF&I had no real interest in sharing the profits with miners; after all, mine workers of the day were not particularly skilled and easily replaceable.

Knowing that they had a weak case, as a last resort the miners called for a strike. In response, CF&I called in their own security team to strong-arm the miners back to work. In a matter of days, they had also used their political influence to pressure Colorado Governor Elias M. Ammons to declare martial law and call in the Colorado National Guard.

It was a disaster. After escalating violence, on April 20, 1914 the National Guard opened fire on the mining camp in Ludlow, Colorado. They set fire to the tents and despite objections from many of their own soldiers, they followed the orders they were given to put down the mining strike at any cost.

In the aftermath, the Red Cross reported finding 26 dead bodies. Among them were two women and 11 children who could not escape and were burned alive while hiding under a cot. The next day the *New York Times* carried this headline: "Women and Children Roasted in Pits of Tent Colony As Flames Destroy It."

Years later in one of the only historical accounts of that day, historian Howard Zinn wrote that it "was the culminating act of perhaps the most violent struggle between corporate power and laboring men in American history."[1] The media called the entire event "The Ludlow Massacre," and the public blamed Rockefeller and corporate greed for the tragedy.

In support of the miners, people picketed outside Rockefeller's office in New York. For the next several months there were more negotiations, mediations, and talks of settlement. They all failed. Finally, the strike was officially called off in December 1914, having accomplished little. As Zinn wrote, "The Union had not won recognition. Sixty-six men, women, and children had been killed. Not one militiaman or mine guard had been indicted for a crime."

Despite their failure to win more labor rights, the whole episode was a major crisis for Rockefeller and his entire family, particularly his son John D. Rockefeller Jr., whom he had put in charge of managing CF&I. It got worse when Rockefeller Jr. went before the U.S. Industrial Relations Commission in 1915 and declared, "There was no Ludlow Massacre." It was clear the family's reputation was tarnished and they would need help to restore it. Luckily, there was a man named Ivy Ledbetter Lee who was perfectly suited for the job.

The Birth of Modern PR

By 1915, Lee had already established quite a reputation for himself. Growing up in Georgia as the son of a Methodist minister, Lee started his career as a journalist for the *New York Times*. Realizing his passion lay elsewhere, in 1905 he founded one of the nation's first public relations firms, Parker and Lee, which used the tagline "Accuracy, Authenticity, and Interest" as their motto.

In 1906, when there was a train accident in Atlantic City, New Jersey, Lee was the one who advised his client, Pennsylvania Railroad,* to issue what is today considered the first press release ever. It shared a public response and disclosed details about the tragedy from the company's point of view. The move was widely seen as a stroke of genius, and even more widely copied.

Writing a press release gave Lee and his client the ability to influence the media before journalists were able to gather facts from elsewhere. Without the Internet or Twitter, this effectively allowed them to control the story. Soon after, Lee was hired full time by Pennsylvania Railroad, making him what his personal archives described as "the first VP-level corporate public relations person."

On the heels of the Ludlow Massacre, Lee was brought in by the Rockefellers to help "manage" the public fury. His first act was to travel to Colorado and speak directly to the people there to understand the situation. Having done that, Lee reported to Rockefeller, "The people

---

*Yes, the same one from *Monopoly!*

of this state have been led to believe by the hostile press that you and your friends are exploiting the state. From friendly sources, I gather this opinion is still widely held."[2]

The fight to restore the Rockefeller reputation, however, did not start well for Lee. In late 1915, he decided to publish some pamphlets, which he titled "Facts Concerning the Struggle in Colorado for Industrial Freedom." They contained many factual "errors" and were widely seen as propaganda. They directly led muckraking journalist Upton Sinclair (who achieved fame for his 1906 exposé of the meat-packing industry, called *The Jungle*) to brand Lee with the nickname "Poison Ivy."

Still, Lee had a gift for the art of influence. Despite his missteps, what he did next was a PR master stroke that is still remembered nearly 100 years later. He advised Rockefeller to carry around dimes in his pocket and hand them out freely to people on the street. A dime (10 U.S. cents) adjusted for inflation was worth approximately 2 dollars by today's standards. For Rockefeller, though, the amount of the money was unimportant.

The simple act of personal charity changed how people saw him, and how history remembered him. He transformed his legacy from a detached billionaire to an engaged, kind, and grandfatherly benefactor of society.

In 2007, PBS aired *The Rockefellers*, a documentary film about the life and times of the Rockefeller family. Despite the fact that the Rockefeller name was despised for many years, the film description noted, "Their contributions transformed America. When he died at age 86, Junior [Rockefeller's son] left his six children and 22 grandchildren an invaluable inheritance: a name which stood not for corporate greed, but for the well-being of mankind."

Thanks to a combination of smart PR and a later dedication from the family to making charitable donations, the Rockefeller family name eventually was no longer a symbol of greed, but rather a leading family in contributing actively to society.

#occupywallstreet

Of course, that was nearly 100 years ago, and times have changed. Today we have big and powerful unions to protect workers' rights. Our average life expectancy has gone up by more than a decade. By law in most countries, monopolies are not allowed. The power to shape entire nations and industries no longer falls into the hands of one individual.

Almost exactly a century after the Ludlow Massacre, in September of 2011, a group of protesters organized by a Canadian activist group called Adbusters set up

> **Even though today is different, some of the problems haven't changed at all.**

a demonstration in New York's Wall Street financial district. Their goal was to protest the unequal distribution of wealth, Wall Street corruption, and the link between politics and money.

Using the rallying cry "Occupy Wall Street" and Twitter hashtags of #occupywallstreet and #ows, the movement started to spread. On October 15th, a global day of solidarity was planned for 951 cities in 82 countries around the world.

It is not exactly the same as the Ludlow Massacre. Though there were moments of violence, very few people lost their lives. What is clear is that the gulf between corporations and the people has remained over the past century. Judging from recent events, it is safe to say that it has grown into a full chasm.

These two events, separated by nearly 100 years, lead to an interesting and important question. If the tension between organizations and individuals has always been present, why hasn't there been more conflict in the last century? The answer may come from turning our attention to something that has become a dirty word: propaganda.

The Propaganda of Revolutions

For nearly as long as humans have recorded history, there have been examples of rulers and their governments using communications to influence or inspire their people. The ancient Romans used large public gatherings where orators would speak publicly to thousands of people about philosophy, religion, and the status and the necessity of the conquests of the Roman Empire.

Since they had no microphone, many orators would begin by learning techniques created by a man named Marcus Fabius Quintilianus for using body gestures to signify meaning. Quintillian even wrote a widely used 12-volume textbook on rhetoric and public oration in AD 95 called *Institutio Oratoria*.

Later in history, the power of these orations would come from storytellers recording famous moments of history to retell them. One example is King Henry V's famous "once more unto the breach" call to arms for his English forces, and countless battle cries from military across the world.

It is no coincidence that many of the most recorded forms of mass communication have come from rulers of countries or leaders of military campaigns. Until very recently, the only real reason to inspire mass belief in an idea was to unite a country or band of revolutionaries to win freedom or conquer another culture. It was only in the last century that this started to shift, and the role of propaganda shifted with it.

In the 1920s, mainly to avoid being "smothered in American culture," the Canadian Radio Broadcasting Commission (CBC) began creating public broadcasting content specifically for the Canadian market. Today the CBC employs nearly 10,000 Canadians and produces original programming on news and current affairs, arts and entertainment, children's programming, and sports.

In 2010, the CBC turned to the historical subject of World War II and created a six-part series called *Love, Hate, and Propaganda* with the mission of showing the central role propaganda played in telling the people what to believe. The introduction to the series went on to describe the war in this way:

> *The first modern war in which all combatants bombarded their citizens with messages . . . they employed truth, half-truths and sometimes outright lies, used powerful symbols and persuasive words to sway entire populations. . . . Every movie house, school, newspaper and radio became a forum for persuasion and manipulation.*

In one particularly telling interview published on the website for the documentary, nonfiction author Antony Beever was asked why propaganda was so important. He responded: "Hatred alone was not enough. What you had to have was a combination of hatred and fear. In a way you could say hatred was the explosive and fear was the detonator." Propaganda was frequently used in this way—to turn fear into action or inaction.

After World War II, there was another form of communications that was also emerging, which would do the same thing—but toward a different objective. Its birthplace was a single street in New York that would soon take on a larger-than-life role in American culture: Madison Avenue.

When Advertising Ruled the World

In 1954, the Leo Burnett Advertising Agency had a challenge before them that only advertising could solve. They had been asked to create a new campaign to reinvent a brand that was launched 30 years earlier exclusively for women with the slogan "Mild as May." Now the parent company, Philip Morris, wanted to make a change.

The early 1950s were a pivotal time for cigarette manufacturers like Philip Morris. In response to growing evidence of the health risks of smoking, they were introducing filtered cigarettes as a "healthier" alternative. The problem was that men considered filtered cigarettes unmasculine and would not buy them. So when Philip Morris approached the team at Leo Burnett, they had a very specific challenge in mind—to turn one of their most popular brands of cigarettes for women, called Marlboro, into a brand for men.

What happened next would become part of advertising history. Leo Burnett launched their new campaign by photographing men in masculine professions like sea captains, athletes, and cowboys smoking the cigarettes . . . and called them all *Marlboro Men*. It was the image of the cowboy more than any other that immediately stuck in people's minds. Launching a nationwide search for an authentic cowboy actor, they found an actor named Darrell Winfield and cast him as the Marlboro Man—a role he would keep for the next 20 years until he retired in the 1980s.

The advertising launched in 1955, and within two years sales to men of the Marlboro brand were up 300 percent. The campaign became a textbook example of the power of advertising in the 1950s to influence public behavior and change the pop culture environment. This was only the beginning.

The 1960s were the true golden age of advertising, directly inspiring the popular television show *Mad Men*. As legendary ad man Jerry Della Famina wrote in the updated introduction to his 1970 cult-classic biography, *From Those Wonderful Folks Who Gave You Pearl Harbor*:

> *The original Mad Men are all dead. Ironically, they died from consuming the products they sold with such gusto. Their lungs went from the cigarettes they were advertising—and smoked by the carton. Their livers melted from all the scotch, gin, and vodka they made famous—and the three martini lunches they enjoyed in the process.*

The upside was that this time of excess did result in many break-through ideas and campaigns. When *AdAge* magazine ad critic Bob Garfield rated the top 100 advertising campaigns of all time, 16 of them came from the 1960s. And many of the other campaigns on the list changed the world around them. Phil Dusenberry, former chairman of BBDO North America, worked with Ronald Reagan in 1984 to help him get reelected. California's legendary "Got Milk?" campaign inspired kids around the country to start drinking more milk. Pepsi-Cola's "Pepsi Generation" defined the attitudes of an entire decade of youth.

Indeed, the golden age of advertising lasted far longer than just the 1960s. The brands dominating that advertising landscape were the same who are around today. And the people creating those ads thrived in their creative roles. "Advertising is the most fun you can have with your clothes on," Della Famina famously quipped. Not only was it fun, but if you spent the right amount and had the right message, you could directly influence public opinion on a mass scale. Then, slowly, over the late 1990s and early 2000s, the Internet came along.

The Mass Perception Principle

For the most part, there used to be a direct *relationship between the money you spent and the perception shift you could buy.* That meant if you spent a lot on buying advertising, you could pretty much shape what people thought about your brand. If you donated large amounts of money to a charity, people would assume you were a good person.

The Mass Perception Principle

More money spent on communications = better brand perception.

Mass media allowed brands to reach lots of people, and there were only two ways that anyone might know or hear something different than what the advertising told them:

1. The media published a negative article or report.
2. Someone had a negative personal experience or heard something negative directly from someone he or she trusted.

In the first case, media could scale to reach a large group of people, but the odds were good that a brand might avoid this sort of negativity because there were still relatively few media outlets. In the second case, word of mouth required personal interaction (often face to face), so it was unlikely to travel far beyond the people directly affected and their own local personal network. Individual voices didn't scale.

Today, the world is different in three important ways:

1. **Media is now fragmented.** What used to be less than a dozen authoritative media outlets has now exploded into millions as the "long tail" of media has become the majority of what people consume. Aside from a few moments like the Olympics or the Super Bowl, there is no mass audience anymore.
2. **Competition is everywhere.** Hardly anyone owns an industry or a category anymore. And competition can come from anywhere. As we will see in Chapter 2, it is also increasingly harder to do anything that is truly unique.
3. **The truth about anything is harder to hide.** While perception was generally easy to shape through marketing, now people have more ways to share their real experiences with products and services through online reviews and publishing content online. As a result, any negativity from a single customer can influence thousands of others in the blink of an eye.

While the Internet has evened the playing field for anyone with a message to share, it has also created a vast ocean of information that never goes away.

Even if the Internet makes it harder to stand out, it is the business world that often gets blamed for the modern believability crisis. As Gary Ruskin, executive director of Ralph Nader's Commercial Alert organization, once said: business may be causing "an epidemic of marketing-related diseases" from smoking and gambling to obesity or diabetes. It is an ugly picture.

When Superman tried to save the world, he was always fighting against an identifiable foe—Lex Luthor. If consumers today were super-heroes, it often seems that business and capitalism has become the evil villains they must rise up against.

Marketing as the Bad Guy

Every movie needs a bad guy. The bad guys ignore social norms. They mistreat the good guys. And they always have ulterior motives to take over the world or make lots of money. Since Rockefeller's time, marketing has been going through a PR crisis of its own. For many outside the industry, any discussion of marketing inevitably brings up discussions about deception, manipulation, exploitation, and all sorts of other evil-sounding words.

Many consumers see marketing as the enemy in their lives—a force trying to interrupt and sell them something by playing on their fears, insecurities, or aspirations.

The corruptive force of marketing is one that branding consultant Martin Lindstrom has spent his career studying and writing about. One of the few people who could be described simultaneously as a consumer advocate *and* a branding consultant, he has published several books written from the perspective of an insider looking at how brands manipulate their customers.

In his popular new book *Brandwashed*, he pulls back the curtain to look at the modern view of marketing as a source of evil:

[Marketers] know more than they ever have before about what inspires us, scares us, soothes us, seduces us. What alleviates our guilt or makes us feel less alone, more connected to the scattered human tribe. What makes us feel more confident, more beloved, more secure, more nostalgic, more spiritually fulfilled. And they know far more about how to use all this information to obscure the truth, manipulate our minds, and persuade us to buy.[3]

And his is not the only book to portray marketers as the enemy, either. Here is just a short list of titles that have come out in the past decade, which raise similar concerns about a world dominated by marketing and communications:

- *Toxic Sludge Is Good for You: Lies, Damn Lies, and the Public Relations Industry* (John Stauber and Sheldon Rampton, 2002)
- *Consumed—How Markets Corrupt Children, Infantilize Adults, and Swallow Citizens Whole* (Benjamin R. Barber, 2007)
- *Obsessive Branding Disorder—The Illusion of Business and the Business of Illusion* (Lucas Conley, 2008)
- *Buyology—Truth and Lies about Why We Buy* (Martin Lindstrom, 2008)
- *Scroogenomics—Why You Shouldn't Buy Presents for the Holidays* (Joel Waldfogel, 2009)
- *The Buying Brain—Secrets for Selling to the Subconscious Mind* (A.K. Pradeep, 2010)
- *Deadly Spin—An Insurance Company Insider Speaks Out on How Corporate PR Is Killing Health Care and Deceiving Americans* (Wendell Potter, 2010)
- *Age of Persuasion—How Marketing Ate Our Culture* (Terry O'Reilly and Mike Tennant, 2011)

The list more than doubles when you start to include all the books that have come out over the past five years casting capitalism itself as the enemy and arguing against everything from accumulating too many things (*Stuff: Compulsive Hoarding and the Meaning of Things,* Gail Steketee, Ph.D. and Randy Frost, Ph.D., 2010) to the rise of corporate power (*Life Inc: How Corporatism Conquered the World, and How We Can Take It Back,* Douglass Rushkoff, 2009).

All of this negativity points to one undeniable conclusion: Marketing has played a central role in creating a culture where people are afraid to trust the media around them. There is plenty of evidence that this growing distrust has already become a full-blown crisis.

Living in the Society of Distrust

Almost every week, there is new research published that documents the expanding trust gap between people and the organizations that they interact with. This is not only a story about people losing trust in business, but also a growing distrust in institutions of all sorts, from the church to government.

In 2011, the 12th annual Edelman Trust Barometer Survey showed that the United States was the only country to see trust in all institutions (business, government, media, and NGOs) decline—a result that mirrored a similar drop from 2008 to 2009 during the global financial crisis. In response to the fundamental question "How much do you trust business to do what is right?" for the second straight year *less than half* the people in the United States rated companies positively.

According to other surveys, the news is even worse. A Gallup survey of confidence in institutions conducted in June of 2011[4] found that only 12 percent of Americans had a "great deal" or "quite a lot" of confidence in the U.S. Congress, only 19 percent in big business, and 26 percent in banks. Perhaps most surprisingly, only 48 percent (less than half) of Americans even declared having either a "great deal" or even "quite a lot" of confidence in a church or an organized religion.

This society of distrust is not only limited to the United States. The 2011 Reader's Digest Trusted European Brands survey presented even more stark results. Based on the responses of more than 33,000 readers in 16 European countries, the survey showed that 3 out of 4 people across Europe did not trust their government, and in Romania it was as low as 6 percent. The same survey reported that advertising topped the list as the least trusted institution (appearing higher than government).

Even Asia, where historically people have been much more likely to trust in businesses and government, this crisis of believability is growing. In the same trust survey from Edelman, 60 percent of respondents from Asia-Pacific surveyed said their trust in business was less today than it was 12 months ago.

Best-selling marketing guru Seth Godin (*All Marketers Are Liars*), as well as legendary author Steven Covey (*7 Habits of Highly Effective People*) both recently used the term "low-trust world" in the titles of their new books to underscore this fact.

Before we can start to discuss how to rebuild this trust, we need to understand some of the core actions that inspire this distrust every day.

> **People around the world have a lower trust in institutions of all forms than ever before. This is the modern believability crisis.**

What Is the Believability Crisis?

The easiest targets to blame for the modern believability crisis are unscrupulous communications professionals. After all, they are often hired as surgeons of spin to expertly slice into our minds and plant ideas with specific agendas. Their expertise in influence is used to modify our behaviors and change our perceptions. A second group you might point the finger toward is greedy investment firms, banks, and companies only motivated by corporate profits. The other clear choice could be politicians more concerned about getting elected or repaying their supporters instead of doing what's right for their respective countries.

The point is, choosing *who* to blame is not really that difficult; there are plenty of groups who rightfully belong on that list. Looking at *why* their actions have led us to where we are is a more interesting question. If we look more deeply at that question, the reasons for the modern believability crisis come down to four basic things:

1. **Real Spin and Actual Lies**—For every nutritional label that declares a product "all natural" or "heart healthy," a consumer's faith in the truth dies just a little bit. The first and most basic reason for distrust is because there are so many companies and people who choose to lie to us either by making misleading claims or simply by hiding the truth. Each time one of these lies erupts into a scandal, for a company or a celebrity or a politician, the public loses a small piece of their trust in the institutions around them. By far, this has been the largest contributor to the modern believability crisis.

2. **Facelessness and Corporate Speak**—We have no personal connection to messages that come from large corporate entities or institutions. As a result we are less likely to believe them. The language
   they use is corporate and inhuman. Their policies are based on
   stupidity or greed. In my first book, *Personality Not Included*, I argued
   that organizations and people needed to find their humanity and
   personality in order to regain trust. Nearly four years later, this has
   become even more important. Faceless organizations and people are
   nearly impossible to like or believe in.

3. **Volume**—There are so many messages that most consumers are
   bombarded with each day that we are all conditioned to automatically distrust everything as a defense mechanism. Marketing firm
   Yankelovich estimates that consumers today encounter from 3,500
   to 5,000 marketing messages per day, vs. 500 to 2,000 in the 1970s.
   When the volume increases exponentially, we all have no choice but
   to start in a default state of distrust. You have to *earn* our trust first,
   with no benefit of the doubt. This is a big fundamental shift that has
   contributed to a basic level of distrust in society.

4. **Consumer Protection**—There are many government agencies
   and third-party groups who have dedicated themselves to some form
   of "consumer protection." Typically, a key part of this involves
   educating consumers to be more savvy. Ironically, this education can
   also lead consumers to automatically distrust organizations because it
   reminds them of how many of the messages they see around them
   are designed to manipulate them in some way, and encourages them
   to be suspicious of everything.

We live in a society where trust is at a premium and harder to earn
than ever before. That's why it is a crisis. The good news is this doesn't
have to be a crisis without a solution.

Solving the Believability Crisis

A world where it is harder for any of us to trust the organizations that
factor into our lives is a world that is broken. For businesses to succeed,
economies to rebound, and people to live happier lives, we need to
change this society of distrust. We need to fix the modern believability
crisis.

Contrary to how it may seem, this is not just a corporate problem to fix. It cannot be us versus them. Dale Carnegie influenced so many people to reshape their views of the world and improve themselves because his books and training courses focused on the intersection of business and life.

There has never been a more important time to focus on this intersection. If we could create more human companies, demand more human politicians and reward the most human ideas, we could start to fix this crisis.

> **When people change, governments, companies, and institutions change with them.**

No matter if you are an entrepreneur, employee, leader, neighbor or community member—the real question is how can you build more believable relationships in an era of distrust?

We see the problem clearly. Now in Chapter 2, we will focus on answering this question, starting with how to navigate something I call the "likeability gap."

CHAPTER 1 IN 60 SECONDS
#BELIEVABILITY CRISIS #LIKEONOMICS

- For all history, rulers and government have used communications to influence people.
- In the golden age of advertising, Madison Avenue made propaganda more commonplace.
- The "mass perception principle" meant that more money = better perception.
- Business and capitalism were seen as the bad guys trying to corrupt us.
- As a result, trust in all institutions has reached an all-time low.
- The modern believability crisis means people are less likely to trust anyone or anything.
- This distrust is fueled by four factors: actual lies, facelessness, volume, and consumer protection.
- We must fix this for businesses to succeed, economies to rebound, and people to live happier lives.
- When people change, companies and governments change with them.

(continued)

(continued)

    Key Takeaway: We are living in a society of distrust where the *modern believability crisis* makes it harder to influence anyone to do anything. In order for businesses to succeed, economies to rebound, and people to build more trusted relationships, this is a crisis that we need to solve immediately.

Navigating the Likeability Gap

What Rwanda, Golf Courses, and *Ocean's Eleven* Can Teach Us about the Decisions We Make

Of all the things I've done, the most vital is coordinating the talents of those who work for us and pointing them toward a certain goal.
—Walt Disney

The first time you meet Scott DiGiammarino, you get the feeling he'd much rather give you a big hug instead of a handshake. Often he'll do exactly that. As a former high school football star who grew up in the affluent Massachusetts sailing town of Marblehead, he had always been one of the least wealthy kids in his neighborhood. Growing up surrounded by wealth, though, gave him a healthy ambition to be a success. It was a drive that would lead him in 1993, at the age of 30, to accept a seemingly impossible job.

That year, he took over as the sales manager for the struggling Mid-Atlantic region of the American Express Financial Advisor Network. At that time, there were 176 individual regions across the United States, and every year they were ranked based on an internal formula that looked at all sorts of criteria such as assets under management, client satisfaction, investment performance, employee retention, and a mix of other metrics. The office he was about to take over was ranked 173rd out of 176.

He knew something drastic had to be done, and he wasted no time trying to take action. In his first month, he reviewed staff performance and attitude. He found the lowest performers and people who had very negative attitudes that were unlikely to change and immediately fired more than half of his 32-person team.

From the beginning, his focus as he recalls was to "create a culture of making principle-based decisions, even when the boss isn't around." It was a lesson his staff learned first-hand one day when he called the full team into an hour-long meeting, after one advisor had been less than completely transparent with a client. His main message: nothing less than full honesty and transparency would be tolerated. If business was going to change, the way the entire team approached their relationships with their customers would have to change first. As Scott would often tell his team, "You need to all feel more empowered to do business with integrity, because integrity always pays off." And it did.

Almost exactly one year after taking over, when the new regional rankings were released, the Mid-Atlantic region had gone from being ranked 173rd to being ranked number one. The rest of the financial advisor community was stunned. It was the first time that such a dramatic turnaround had ever been seen. Still, most people just figured it was beginners' luck, or the benefit of cleaning house and getting new staff.

Scott wasn't ready to quit, though. Through the entire second year, Scott reminded his staff that going from worst to first was easy. It was staying on top that would be hard. What they did next would not only surprise their peers again, it would make their region the most successful in the history of the company.

For 13 of the next 15 years, the office maintained that number one spot—until Scott finally decided to retire from his role at Amex in 2008 to start his own company. How had his region managed one of the most stunning turnarounds in company history, and then sustained it year after year for a decade and a half?

The Movie Man

It turns out American Express wanted to know the answer to that question as well. Their first step was to hire management consulting firm McKinsey to find out. Following their standard process, McKinsey sent in a team of consultants to spend weeks studying Scott and his staff to uncover their secrets. The research was exhaustive.

They looked at every aspect of performance, from the office structure to the incentive system used for employees. They grilled Scott about his management methods. They tested the attitude and performance of his employees. They created surveys to distribute to partners and even conducted face-to-face interviews with customers.

After all this research, they produced a comprehensive report that pointed to a single puzzling conclusion: Scott managed to get the best performance from his employees because they *cared* the most about delivering great results. Unlike many other regional managers, he was somehow able to inspire his team to try harder and had best in class employee management year after year. There was an immense source of pride in being part of the team that was at the top, and that pride related to the work that they did.

It wasn't the sort of conclusion that McKinsey consultants like to end up with. After all, given such long-lasting success, there must be something specific that set that region apart, but every obvious rationale had failed.

Was Scott an extraordinarily gifted recruiter of great talent? No, after reviewing his team, they found no evidence that the people there were inherently more talented than the people in any other region across the network.

Was their region inherently better or bigger? No, the results per advisor and client were still better even when corrected for size.

Were they somehow cheating or getting measured on different criteria? Again, the team came up empty-handed—without an explanation.

If it wasn't talent or an unfair advantage or cheating, what could it be? Buried within the report, the McKinsey team *had* uncovered one particularly unique thing that Scott did religiously to connect with and motivate his staff. Every morning he would create an inspirational message to send out to his staff along with a video clip from a Hollywood film. Scott was a huge film buff and loved using movies to explain concepts.

Early in his role at Amex, Scott realized that with such a geographically spread out team, he could never be everywhere at once. And yet, he still needed to motivate and connect with his team members spread across multiple office locations.

His daily messages of inspiration were how he managed to do it. One day, influenced by his football past, he would play a scene from the movie *Rudy*. Then he would show the final scene from the Oscar-winning film *Dead Poets Society*, where students stand on their desks and pledge their support for their professor, played by Robin Williams. After showing a clip like that, he would ask his team leaders, "What are you doing that would make your staff stand on their desks for you?"

Over time, Scott built up a list of 200 qualities that he wanted to inspire in his staff. It included everything from being more compassionate and genuinely caring to consistently going above and beyond. Throughout, he would use movies as a shared language to encourage people to take more responsibility and ownership over their roles. When a staff member came to him with a problem, for example, he would ask them to imagine how Tom Hanks's character in *Castaway* might handle it. Movies brought his lessons to life and helped empower his staff to solve their own problems.

After each video, staff engagement would go way up. People started sharing these clips and the recorded messages from Scott. They would respond and engage with him virtually. One of the most basic and important metrics in the financial services industry was employee retention. Scott knew that if he could keep a good financial advisor for four years, he would keep 97 percent of them long term. And keeping your best employees for the long term is the most important factor in building a successful services based business. Thanks to his ability to connect with his teams and inspire them, his employee retention rate was off the charts compared with other regions.

The formula for success could almost write itself at this point. Keep your best people for longer; they will perform better and grow the business, and you will continue to succeed. Could it be that something as simple as inspirational snippets of video was the explanation for

Scott's success? The McKinsey report was forced to conclude that it just might be, and that was the best they could do.

As soon as the report was shared with the Amex management team, it turned Scott into something of an internal rock star. Deciding they needed more of his philosophy across their entire organization, Scott was given an internal television show to host. He started traveling around the country to speak at other Amex offices. More teams of consultants and internal offices sent their own people to visit Scott's offices to see how they did it, prompting his assistant at the time to joke that their offices sometimes felt "like a motel" with all these people coming in and out.

As he would later share, his most important guiding belief was also his simplest: "If I can help my team personally," he would say, "they'll give me their best efforts professionally." When he finally left Amex in 2008, his video idea became the basis for a new business called ReelPotential, which now helps brands of all sizes to create these inspiration programs based on officially licensed Hollywood films. To this day, his track record of success in building a successful team of financial advisors has been unmatched.

What Business Are You In?

When you think about businesses like financial advisors, it is probably not hard to imagine that personal relationships really matter. If your staff is highly motivated and inspired, *of course* you can get the best performance from them. But how much do personal relationships really matter when you are trying to sell someone a commodity that anyone might sell—like a can of Coke?

In 2011, as part of a feature that involved interviewing dozens of CEOs, Adi Ignatious, the editor of the *Harvard Business Review*, spoke with the CEO of Coca-Cola, Muhtar Kent, about the challenges facing Coke. The conversation ranged from Coke's growing investment in social media (moving from 3 percent to 20 percent of their overall media spend), to how they manage the world's largest Facebook brand page with over 40 million fans. They touched on sustainability and spoke of Coke's impact on the world.

Near the end of the interview, Ignatius asked a pointed question about Kent's decision to spend a significant part of his time actually visiting real supermarkets to be with customers. Surely a CEO of a large global brand like Coke would have better things to do than visit stores around the world that sell Coke? This was his response:

> It's important to be seen, because we are a people business. We're one of the largest private employers in the world, and it's important that all our people who touch customers be motivated and feel good about what they're doing. It's about being proud of what you're doing.

Wait a second, Coke is *a people business? Don't they just sell cans of soda?* Though it may sound odd on the surface, what Kent and other great leaders realize is that nearly every business in the world is actually a people business on a basic level. It is people who make the biggest contribution to whether a business is a success or a failure. And as Scott DiGiammarino and Muhtar Kent both know, the bad news is that those people aren't nearly as engaged as anyone would like.

The Engagement Problem

In 2007, the global professional services and recruiting firm Towers Perrin conducted a survey of nearly 90,000 employees in 18 countries around the world. The aim, as it was every year, was to spot some trends in how satisfied employees were with their jobs and what they were thinking. Unlike many other surveys, this was global and reported back on countries individually in the results. What they learned was concerning: The global workforce is *not* engaged.

Only one out of five workers on the job was giving what the global survey called "full discretionary effort" on the job.

In English, this meant that only close to 20 percent of an average professional workforce was actually trying as hard as they could to produce quality work. More disturbingly, nearly 4 out of 10 (38 percent) were described as what the study called "disenchanted or disengaged."

Ironically, the study also found that despite the pitifully low levels of engagement, employees worldwide *wanted* to give more, but were being held back for some reason. The majority of the reasons did not come down to compensation, but rather the employee's relationship with the organization, its leadership, and their work experience.

It is no wonder that in 2011, a book with the title *How to Work for an Idiot* was a *New York Times* best seller. Our relationship with work is rarely one that inspires a "full discretionary effort." There are plenty of people who don't necessarily love what they do, and therefore put in the effort required but not much more.

The gap between what organizations are able to inspire their employees to do and what those same employees are capable of doing is considerable. It was enough to explain why Scott's focus on motivating his team of financial advisors helped them consistently rank higher than most of their peers across the country.

It is also why business media and culture today celebrate the few companies like Zappos who have focused on creating a dynamic and incentive-rich culture, where people are empowered to do great work and act on their own ideas. Creating more engagement among employees requires a more direct and human connection.

When you have a real human connection, you can focus on the three most important elements of motivation:

1. **Purpose**—answering the all important question of why something should matter and is worth doing or believing in.
2. **Empowerment**—giving people a sense that they have influence to control their own actions and are trusted to do things to the best of their ability without needing permission for everything.
3. **Appreciation**—when people feel that what they do is important and they are thanked for their efforts, they are more likely to be motivated to do more and perform better.

The principle that lies underneath each of these elements is simple. People are inspired and get engaged because of leaders who can connect with them personally. This personal connection inspires trust. One of the most powerful stories that proves this is the dramatic 17-year reversal of fortunes for a country that was once known mainly for its violent ethnic wars.

The Reinvention of Rwanda

In the span of 100 days in 1994, over a million people died in an ethnic war in Rwanda while the world sat back and did nothing. It was one of the darkest moments in human history, but it was also a turning point, bringing a rebel army to power that was led by a man named Paul Kagame. For the next 17 years, he would remain president of Rwanda and lead his country in an unprecedented revival that CNN called "Africa's biggest success story."

Though South Africa gets a lot of well-earned media attention for its recent prosperity, it has a lot of natural benefits that Rwanda never had. Plentiful coastline, a large and connected immigrant population, and vast natural mines of diamonds. Rwanda, in contrast, is a mountainous country about the size of Maryland and has the highest population density in sub-Saharan Africa. As leader of a land-locked country in Eastern Africa, Kagame was quick to realize that it would be Rwanda's ability to build relationships with others around the continent would be crucial.

He focused on encouraging more Rwandans to become business-people and opened up trade routes with neighboring countries like Congo and Tanzania. He sent teams of people on fact-finding missions to places like Singapore to learn from their examples about how they managed to create reputations and desirable qualities to grow their economies. And he personally went out and made friends.

He invited Costco CEO Jim Sinegal to visit Rwanda, and struck a deal in which Costco began purchasing about 25 percent of the country's premium coffee crop. Sinegal introduced him to then Starbuck CEO Howard Schultz who later agreed to become the country's second top buyer. Kagame established a well-connected circle of business leaders to join his "Presidential Advisory Council" and began to see even more successes.

In 2009, the country struck a deal to invest $100 million to lay fiberoptic cable that rivals most Western nations and would make Rwanda one of the most connected countries in Africa. Most importantly, Kagame built and used his direct connection to some of the most influential people in the world to make sure they were not only invested in the country, but that they also had a front-row seat to watch the transformation of Rwanda.

It has worked. Since 2004, the GDP for the country has risen every year. It is now listed by the World Bank among the top 50 countries in the world to do business, the same list where they used to be ranked 150th. Most interestingly, according to the World Bank's Doing Business Survey, they are now tied with the United States as the ninth easiest country in which to do business.

As Clet Niyikiza, a successful drug researcher who was living in the United States and who agreed to join the President's Advisory Council, noted, "[President Kagame] wanted advocates for the country to the rest of the world . . . the idea was to do that through relationships." These relationships were a necessity. None of the growth in reputation that Rwanda has enjoyed would have happened without Kagame's ability to make personal connections.

For years, the world stood by as over a million people were massacred. Today, businesses like Costco and Starbucks actively buy from the country. A new Marriott hotel is being constructed in Kigali (the capital). In his annual address to the nation in 2011, President Kagame promised, "Those in need of healthcare will have easy access to it and all Rwandan children will be able to go to school in 2012."

What turned Rwanda's fortunes around was Paul Kagame's ability to encourage influential leaders to act to support his vision and the country because they *wanted* to. But what is that single quality that matters so much when it comes to inspiring people through leadership? If any of us were asked to guess what it might be, our responses would be predictable. Passionate. Innovative. Bold. Visionary.

In reality, it turns out that the ability to successfully build a profitable company or reinvent a nation comes down to a more surprising quality. And, as management consultant and best-selling author of *Good to Great* Jim Collins uncovered after years of research, it is not a quality that anyone would ever guess.

Humility Wanted

Though he didn't realize it at the time, a simple question during a dinner conversation would engross Jim Collins for more than five years of his life.

His critically acclaimed first book, *Built to Last*, investigated what made a company visionary. Visionary companies, as Collins defined them, were those that endured for generations and made an impact on the world around them. It wasn't just about profits, though all of his examples were indeed highly profitable. Instead, the companies he researched—Ford, American Express, Walt Disney, Sony, and Boeing (to name just a few)—had a combination of "cult-like cultures" and ideologies that focused on more than profits.

The question his dinner companion would ask that night was whether great companies *required* larger-than-life leaders like Walt Disney or Henry Ford, or whether companies might be able to *learn* to be great? Tackling this question, Collins methodically studied and researched for nearly five years to find the answer before writing his second book, *Good to Great*. In that time, he uncovered many surprising truths about the nature of success, leadership, and vision.

At the top of the list was the discovery of a type of leader he termed a "Level 5 Executive." Level 5 Executives, according to Collins's research, were not larger-than-life personalities. Instead, they were leaders who spent more time "looking out the window than looking in the mirror." They were modest and resolved and humble.

Humble? That certainly doesn't seem to describe many modern leaders who are regularly noted as being among the most successful in the world. Yet, when looking at hundreds of other companies for comparison, Collins found that in more than two-thirds of them a "gargantuan personal ego contributed to the demise or continued mediocrity of the company."[1]

The 11 leaders profiled as the heads of *Good to Great* companies are hardly household names. Here are a few that made the list: Jim Herring, Colman Mockler, and Darwin E. Smith. Have you even heard of any of them? Yet each was wildly successful in building an enduring and great business: Kroger (Herring), Gillette (Mockler), and Kimberly-Clark (Smith). So if it is not about being the most inspirational or visionary leader, then what does it take?

The conclusion Collins reached focused on the extraordinary drive that Level 5 leaders possessed. He wrote that they are "fanatically driven, infected with an incurable need to produce results."[2] Rather than focusing on what they will get, they combine professional will with personal humility in order to do whatever they need to do toward build an enduring, great company.

The drive component of success and the need to be extraordinarily driven certainly shouldn't be a surprise to anyone. But why was humility such a critical factor? After all, if people follow great vision and the job of a CEO is to make big decisions and inspire staff, surely there are plenty of other more important qualities? It is no secret that humble people tend to be more likeable. What is interesting is just how important that likeability is to inspiring people to actually *do something*.

The Likeability Gap

All people and all situations are not created equal. There is a greater understanding today among business professionals that simply offering good service or a decent product is not enough. To get people to come back, you need more than just *satisfaction*. Part of the reason why is because just being satisfied is not remarkable, and people don't typically talk about an experience unless it is either remarkably good or remarkably bad. And even then, it is much easier to get them to vent about a bad experience, especially online.

It was a point that author and Nestlé executive Pete Blackshaw aptly wrote about in his 2009 book, *Satisfied Customers Tell Three Friends, Angry Customers Tell 3,000*.

Over and over, the same pattern turns out to be true. Social media offers an easy outlet for the unhappy, but people sharing positivity is far more rare. This is not just a social media problem, either. The most popular sentiment toward anything isn't love or hate—it is indifference.

Consider the following questions:

- When you have a great meal, why do you choose to go online to post a review for some restaurants and not for others?
- When asked by a colleague or friend of a friend on LinkedIn for help in finding a job, which people do you go out of your way to recommend and forward their details to your HR person?
- If you work in a role where you provide any type of service to customers, which customers do you work hardest to provide good service for?

All of these are common choices that many of us face in our daily lives. They are all a matter of degrees. *How much* would you go out of your way for someone or something? That is a choice we all make, and those choices are what fuel many of our interactions with others.

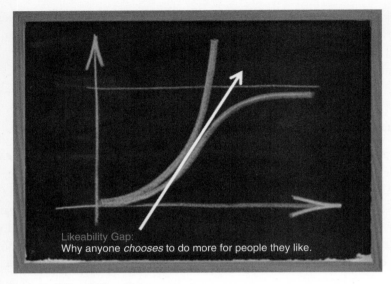

Likeability Gap:
Why anyone *chooses* to do more for people they like.

Figure 2.1   Likeability Gap

The answer comes down to something called the *Likeability Gap* (see Figure 2.1).

> The Likeability Gap describes the difference between what someone decides to do because they *have to*, and what they do because they *want to*.

When you are likeable, you can bridge this gap, and the benefits are almost endless. More likeable businesses hold on to their best employees longer. More likeable people hear about the best job openings first. For more likeable people, the things many of us attribute to good luck just seem to happen. Many of the examples you'll find in this book are of people and companies that have managed to bridge this likeability gap in order to find their success.

To see why the likeability gap is such a powerful force in our lives and how we make decisions, let's look at a few examples of the principle in action, beginning with the story of a guy who started his career doing something many people wouldn't even consider—and continuing to do it for 20 years.

The Toilet Business

Today, Tim Kerin jokes about getting his start in business by cleaning toilets. He can afford to. He runs a company called Falcon Crest, which is one of the most successful commercial cleaning and contracting businesses in the Washington, DC, region. For more than five years, his company was the official cleaning partner for Redskins Stadium, and works with many of the largest businesses in the DC area.

In 15 years of business, he has had his fair share of experience with the power of likeability, and seen plenty of situations where it was missing. He has survived overcharging attorneys, being stiffed more than $60,000 by a client, almost going bankrupt, losing an unemployment case to an employee with a sixth-grade education, and managing to still build a profitable business.

Having gone through most of this early in his business career, he now spends a day a week teaching aspiring entrepreneurs about the reality of running your own business. At over six feet tall with a deep voice, when he tells you how the world works, you are likely to listen. His most important lesson he often shares is about the unexpected power of being likeable.

One of his favorite examples is how a personal connection put him in contact with the procurement manager for Boeing, who was looking for a small contractor to paint some conference rooms with dry erase paint so they could use the walls for meetings. It was a small job, but it offered a foot in the door. Over the years that small piece of work has grown into more than $1 million of contracting work for Boeing every year.

Almost all of us have a story like this to tell. We might attribute it to unexpected strokes of good luck. Or we say we just knew the right person at the right time. Usually, the idea of who we meet within our social networks and how they make an impact on our lives is hard to explain in concrete terms. Even professionals who study human interactions have struggled for decades to do it.

One of the most popular theories to explain this is one that has been cited more than 20,000 times over the past 40 years (according to Google Scholar), written by a sociologist named Mark Granovetter. In 1973, he first published a paper called "The Strength of Weak Ties" to offer an intriguing new explanation for why the benefits of social networks might be quite so unpredictable.

Understanding Weak Ties

If you had to think about the last three jobs you have held in your career, how did you get them? Did you search exhaustively online for an opening and send in a resume to a generic HR e-mail address? Was it through an online job opening or a listing in a newspaper?

No—most of us would credit some kind of personal connection with helping us to get into an opportunity and eventually find our next job. This is quite common. A Gallup poll of job seekers conducted in 2008 found that the number one source that job seekers turned to was friends and family, and it was also among the most effective methods for actually landing a new job.

That alone is not particularly new information. Your relationship to the friends and family who tend to introduce you to your next job, though, may surprise you. In his study, Granovetter conducted a random sampling of professional, technical, and managerial workers who had recently changed jobs in the Boston area. He asked them how often they *saw* the contact who helped them find their new role. Using this as a metric for the strength of their social ties to one another, he found that only 16.7 percent of people saw their contact "often."

The rest reported either occasionally (55.6 percent) or rarely (28.8 percent) seeing their contact. For most of us, this would seem to be a counterintuitive result. After all, your closest connections should be the ones most likely to help you find a new job, right? Instead, Granovetter proposed that your "weak ties" (the less familiar connections) may be even more important when it comes to situations like finding a new job.

The fact is your weak ties are more likely to travel in social circles outside your own. As a result, they are also more likely to have access to information that your inner circle of friends might not have, such as interesting and new potential jobs.

The people who are able to foster the most meaningful weak ties, Granovetter concluded, are also the ones who are able to earn trust more effectively, because weak ties will vouch for them and help convince any skeptics that they are indeed trustworthy.

There is a simple connection to make here: The likeability gap can also explain how some people are able to build more weak ties while others aren't.

Whether you consider the impact of weak ties or strong ties, the fact is that together they lead to the most profitable connections and finding your next job.

> **Being likeable helps you to form weak ties as well as strong ties much more effectively, and both are extremely valuable.**

They even might explain why so many million–dollar deals seem to be done on a golf course.

Golf and the Likeability Gap

Bill Storer runs what might be one of the most unique training organizations in the world. For more than a decade, the former AT&T executive has been delivering a half–day seminar for executives on how to do business on the golf course. It is a smart business to be in. While golf itself has seen declining participation over the past decade, there are still almost 16,000 golf courses across the United States, with golfers playing nearly half a billion rounds of golf each year.[3]

More importantly, over the last century golf has become a symbol of networking and leisure for affluent business professionals around the world. Real estate developer and reality show star Donald Trump is one of the many business professionals who credits his time on the golf course to building business relationships and closing deals:

> *I have done many deals on the golf course. You learn a lot about people on the golf course. For me, if I see someone moving the ball then the probability is that they will move the ball in business. And then there are guys that would never ever think of moving a ball and they are that way in life, too.*[4]

As Storer says when pitching the importance of his seminars on business golf, "There is no better way to further a relationship than to spend six hours in a golf cart with somebody. You can't sit with someone in a lunch room or a board room and develop a relationship like you can on the golf course."[5] Perhaps no moment illustrates this better than the story of Archie Williams, the founder of Roxbury Technology, a manufacturer of toner cartridges.

Back in 1989, Boston was a city divided by lingering racial tensions from a busing crisis in the 1970s. One side effect of this tension was that black and white business owners rarely found opportunities to work together. Community volunteer Diddy Cullinane worked with her husband, John, that year to create an event sponsored by Catholic Charities to bring people together. Featuring comedian Bill Cosby, the event was a big success—a lightning rod for what might be possible if communities could collaborate more.

Following the event, Cullinane put together something she called the Black & White on Green Golf Tournament as a chance for business owners to get together and network in a casual and professional way. It was from this golf tournament that the unlikely partnership between Archie Williams and a man named Thomas Stemberg would emerge.

Thomas Stemberg was the founder of Staples, Inc., and over a few rounds of golf the two men created the perfect idea for a business partnership. Williams would make and distribute the toner cartridges and Staples would sell them through their stores. Though Williams tragically passed away in 2002, just months before the deal would start, his daughter Beth picked up where he left off and turned his dream into a reality.

When interviewed about the experience years later, Stemberg would say, "We haven't ended racism in Boston but we have made a chink in the armor. The work left to be done perhaps requires a more subtle approach than getting people in the room."

The experience did indeed lead to many other organizations being created over the next decade to create more opportunities for col- laboration far beyond the golf tournament. The story of Stemberg and Williams an example of the likeability gap at work: where better personal relationships often lead to stronger business collaboration and results.

Why Relationships Are *Not* about Networking

Many people might call this golf example and the act of building mean- ingful relationships in general an example of the importance of net- working. *Building real and meaningful relationships is not the same thing as networking.* Networking is often described as a sport. You need to keep score of who you meet. The ultimate goal is always to make sure to connect with as many people as you can, and have your elevator pitch ready to deliver in 10 seconds or less. There are now speed networking events available all over the world—a way to make sure that you never "waste" more than about three minutes on a conversation that won't directly help you in some way.

As a result of the way we often turn the act of meeting people into a business neces-

Networking needs to die.

sity, networking is on that unfortunate list of things that people learn they *must* do in order to be successful. It is often described as a rite of passage and necessary evil to rising up in business, with scores of books, training courses, and seminars dedicated to teaching you how to be a better networker. It is now even part of the required curriculum at many business schools. The problem with networking, as best-selling author Keith Ferrazzi says, is that it focuses you on keeping score of who you help and what they should owe you in return.

We can all recall a moment when we met some-one who clearly was trying to get to know us only as a strategy for being able to sell

Relationships don't work when you measure them on a scorecard.

us something or ask us for a favor later. No one likes those people.

As Ferrazzi writes: "We vote for the people we like and respect. Great companies are built by CEOs who inspire love and admiration. In today's world, mean guys finish last."[6]

One man who is often used as a case study for this (though he passed away in 2007) is former advertising executive and White House aide Jack Valenti, who became head of the Motion Picture Association of America (MPAA) in 1966 and remained at its head for nearly 40 years. During that time, the industry created the parental movie rating system, and more recently led the charge to protect digital copyright of motion pictures in a digital and streaming world.

Valenti's skills in building relationships with politicians and members of Congress, and his loyalty to friends even in the face of unwanted publicity, was legendary. As he would often say, "In a political struggle, never get personal—else the dagger digs too deep." He was a Texas man, known for his colorful expressions.

What Valenti knew intuitively was that the power of his personal relationships made people much more likely to understand and be sympathetic toward his point of view and be open to helping support him and the efforts of the MPAA. He was a master at navigating the likeability gap.

Valenti also worked in an industry where the importance of bridging the likeability gap comes up every day. Especially if your challenge happens to be convincing a dozen of Hollywood's most famous stars to take a big pay cut.

Getting Julia Roberts

When self-made Hollywood agent and movie producer Jerry Weintraub decided to remake the old Frank Sinatra film *Ocean's Eleven* in 1998, he had the crazy idea to get a dozen of the hottest actors in the business at the time to all agree to be part of a film. Everyone in the industry had told him the idea was impossible. But Weintraub started simple. He went to two friends he knew and respected—actor George Clooney and director Stephen Soderbergh—and convinced them both to agree to be part of this film.

Even with those two on board, everyone knew that no film (even one with a big budget) could afford to pay millions of dollars each to a cast of a dozen actors all used to being in a leading role. As Weintraub recalls in his personal memoir, *When I Stop Talking, You'll Know I'm Dead*, getting the rest of the actors was all thanks to the relationships and likeability of Clooney and Soderbergh.

The duo personally went to each star and helped convince them to be part of the ensemble cast for a fraction of what they would usually make per film. When they sent the script to Julia Roberts (who usually gets $20 million per movie), they attached a 20-dollar-bill along with a note that said, "We know you get 20 for a movie, but you will have to work for a little less on this one." She agreed to do it, and they quickly also signed Andy Garcia, Matt Damon, Don Cheadle, and Brad Pitt.

When asked later why they agreed, each said a personal relationship was the most important thing. They just liked each other enough to *want* to be part of a unique project, regardless of the money, and the movie got made.

As we have seen so far in this chapter, people and personal relationships matter in every situation—from trying to make a movie to building a business cleaning toilets. But there is still one question left to answer, and it is an important one.

In all of this focus on being more likeable, how important is it to have a good product or service or idea? If you lived in an ideal world, everything you said and every product you were trying to sell would have a "blue ocean"—an open marketplace where you filled a need that no one else was filling. Of course everyone should aim for originality. Every product should be a year ahead of its competitors, like the iPad. Every job you shoot for should be a perfect fit for your skills. Every service should be unlike anything anyone else might offer.

Counting on originality, however, isn't always the best bet. Standing out based on being completely different from everything else around isn't just hard—in some cases it may be fairly close to impossible. The reason why comes down to the fact that we are in what you might call the "age of equivalence."

The Age of Equivalence

Facebook is not the most popular social networking site in Russia, and according to many expert analysts, it may never be. Instead, Russians have their own regionally built social network

The Age of Equivalence describes a time when almost every product or service will have a competitor (over time) that will become nearly indistinguishable from the original.

called Vkontakte (or "in contact"), which has close to 120 million users (as of early 2012) and is the leading site in Europe in terms of user visits, page views, and the amount of data transfers per day.

The fact that there is a customized Russian-language social network is not particularly surprising, but if you spent any time looking at Vkontakte, you would notice one very startling fact—it *looks* almost exactly like Facebook.

Much of the functionality is the same, the way the network allows you to connect with friends is similar, and even the bold white letters of the logo on a blue background remind you of Facebook's logo. In fact, it is a "Facebook clone," and there are many other examples of clones with social networking sites around the world.

In China, a site called Weibo has done the same thing to Twitter, cloning much of its functionality and becoming the leading microblogging site in China, nearly twice the size of Twitter. And this trend is bigger than just cloned versions of social media sites, as well.

Some companies even manage to clone *their own* products so effectively they may not even need competition. Last year, when I purchased a computer monitor from Samsung, I chose two products to compare. They had identical model numbers, but one had "HD" at the end of the number and the other had "BD"—they were almost the same except a few plugs at the back. There were four other models in the same size with similar features that I could also have chosen.

Unfortunately, this type of duplication has become commonplace:

- Sony sells nine different models of 46-inch television sets in the United States.
- Pepsi makes 14 flavors of SoBe Lifewater, including SoBe Lifewater Strawberry Dragonfruit, SoBe Lifewater Strawberry Kiwi, and SoBe Lifewater B-Energy Strawberry Apricot. And just in case Lifewater is not your thing, SoBe Smooth Strawberry Banana or SoBe Sugar-Free Adrenaline Rush are always available.
- When you walk into a pharmacy to purchase a painkiller, you are faced with a choice of either Tylenol or a more generic "acetaminophen." Pharmacologically, they are identical.
- A typical Walmart has more than 100,000 products, and the inventory changes regularly.
- In 2004, two different reality TV shows featured women who could help struggling parents to discipline their out of control children. One was called *Nanny 911*, the other *SuperNanny*. The same year, *Trading Spouses* and *WifeSwap* both premiered within weeks of each other (you can guess the premise behind both of those reality shows).
- Mutual funds can appear to be the same in terms of the investments they carry and only really vary in terms of particulars like management fees and performance.

Clearly, it has become harder for anyone to produce a product, service, or idea that is completely original. So in a world where it is so hard to stand out, how can we rediscover our own originality in anything we want to accomplish?

How Originality Died—and How We Can Get It Back

The American poet and activist Audre Lorde is credited with the famous saying: "There are no new ideas. There are only new ways of making them felt." The saying came to my mind several years ago, while I was attending the South By Southwest (SXSW) Music, Film, and Interactive Festival—a several-week-long celebration of arts, music, film, and business held in Austin, Texas.

That year a panel had been put together to look at the rise of China in the global marketplace, and featured an appealing title: "Social Media and China: It's Not What You Think." One of the lessons shared on the panel was that the Chinese model of innovation had a very fundamental difference from the one used in many other parts of the world. Using a model the panelists called the "5 Cs of Chinese Innovation," the first "C" stood for a surprising principle: copy. Most innovative ideas in China, the panel concluded, always started with a decision to copy and build from something that had already been done and try to improve it.

It was just one example of how innovation itself might be changing in response to the world around us. Consider, for example, the three critical factors driving the age of equivalence:

1. **Speed**—When faced with the deadline-driven pressures of business, the easiest thing isn't to create something entirely original but rather to refine something that already exists. This is the inspiration for the Chinese model of innovation mentioned above. Unfortunately, it often leads to marginal differences and products that appear on the surface to be mostly the same.
2. **Lower Barriers of Entry**—There was a time where you needed to have specific connections with manufacturing groups, lots of financing, and an official presence in order to launch a business.

Now people can work virtually, find an outsourced manufacturer, and create and launch new products in record times. It is only a very small handful of industries (such as aviation or biomedical engineering) where larger barriers to entry still exist.

3. **Reverse Engineering**—Almost before any device hits the store shelves, there are teams of engineers looking at its inner workings to dissect and recreate it. To some degree, this leads to illegal activities like piracy or the global counterfeit market for generic drugs. In other cases, this simply means companies can improve their competitive products and release them rapidly after the market leader comes out.

The sad truth is, in many cases, things are harder and harder to differentiate from one another because they *actually aren't that different*. It points to a big disconnection between the theory of strategy and the reality of business. How does the theory of differentiation work in a world where any competitive advantage can be erased almost overnight by a competitor willing to watch and learn from your example and improve upon it in real time?

The Differentiation Ideal

The most obvious way to avoid becoming a mere clone of your competition is to truly do a better job of differentiating by actually *being* different. Professor Youngme Moon is one of the most popular teachers at Harvard Business School. In 2010, she published a brilliant book called *Different*.

In the book, she looks at brands that manage to do this and proposes a unique and important theory as to why differentiation happens. Brands like IKEA or Google, which she uses as great examples of differentiators, have the ability to be, as she calls it, "lopsided." Instead of trying to be all things to all people, they find a way to double down on the things that they are great at and remain unapologetic about the things that they don't do well.

The most powerful thing about reading *Different* is that it offers its own lopsided academic view of the rationale for focusing on being different. Professor Moon doesn't apologize for her idealism, either. Yet, throughout the book it is clear that very small few brands are able to meet this ideal. It doesn't mean that we all shouldn't try for truly being different, but what if there was a way to succeed even if you couldn't live up to the ideal of being completely different?

The upside of this is that you might fall short on creating true differentiation, but still find an audience. The reason for this is clear if you look at the reality of how we buy products, as well as how we choose which people to believe or follow.

Differentiation is hard to accomplish, and even harder to maintain. In a world where almost any product or idea can be copied relatively quickly, the only competitive edge that lasts is what you can build based on relationships.

The fact is we don't always need (or get) something that is completely unique. In fact, if there ever was a force that could counteract this need to be different in order to stand out, it would be the strength of a personal connection.

Here's a personal example. The Guatemalan coffee that I buy from my local farmer's market really doesn't taste that different from the coffee I could buy at my local grocery store. The package size is the same, and it is actually more work for me to wait until Saturday and then drive to the farmer's market to buy the coffee. Yet, every weekend in the summer I do exactly that. Why? Because I have a personal connection with Mimi, the lady who sells it.

Mimi has family in Guatemala who help her source and import the coffee. She knows the names of my kids. She always has a coffee waiting for me at the stall along with the bag of beans that I buy, and all of that makes the extra effort and expense worth it. How many other things we buy fall into exactly the same category? Certainly any commodity product that is the same at any retail location. As well as commodity services which are nearly indistinguishable from one another (getting your car washed, for example).

Having a game-changing product or innovation will always matter. As long as no one else is selling the iPad, or the Walkman, or vitamin-enriched water, or ready-to-assemble furniture, you have a competitive advantage. If no one else knows how to translate documents from Swahili into Swedish, or fly a rescue helicopter into the mountains, you can probably charge any fee you want for those services because they are desperately needed. Those situations, though, are relatively rare in our daily lives and only work in the short term.

In the long term, the only thing that can help the most successful organizations and people differentiate is based on their human elements, as well as what they sell or what they say.

The Likeability Gap and the World

This book (and this chapter in particular) offers a very specific view of the world. It is a people-centric view. We learned that the people who are able to inspire their teams to give the extra effort are the ones who are able to make a connection on a human level. We saw that engagement can be a choice, and getting the people around you to *choose* to do more is the surest path to being more successful.

The Likeability Gap is a simple principle that can often mean the difference between success and failure. It is why people who manage to forge new relationships with others based on "weak ties" are more successful at finding a new job and starting social movements. It explains the often spoken about phenomenon of big deals getting done on golf courses and people deciding instantly based on a sales pitch and meeting whether they will buy a product or not, regardless of a product's features.

Still, the argument is not complete without taking a hard look at how you might describe (and measure!) the real importance and impact of likeability on everything from helping a great idea survive to helping a small business to prosper. To do that, we will turn our attention in the next chapter to the three favorite letters for analytical businesspeople—ROI—and everything we understand (and misunderstand) about it.

CHAPTER 2 IN 60 SECONDS
#LIKEABILITYGAP #LIKEONOMICS

- We live in a world where simply having a good product or service isn't enough.
- No matter what they sell, every business in the world is a people business on some level.
- Only 20 percent of the average workforce is fully engaged, but people want to do more.

- The secret to motivating people is based on three elements: purpose, empowerment, and appreciation.
- Leaders who are able to motivate best are driven, humble, and likeable.
- The Likeability Gap describes the difference between what someone does because they *have* to and what they do because they *want* to.
- Building meaningful relationships is the key, but it's not about networking or keeping score.
- Differentiation of products or services is harder than ever, because most things can be copied fast.
- The most successful organizations and people differentiate on more than what they sell.

Key Takeaway: The Likeability Gap describes the difference between what people do because they *have* to, and what they do because they *want* to. In a world where just having a good product or service isn't enough, the likeability gap explains success and failure.

The ROI of Likeability

Why Spreadsheets Need to Die, Websites Stink, and Likeable Politicians Always Win

How does one measure the success of a museum?
—J. Paul Getty, American Industrialist and Art Collector

In 1985, the state of Tennessee launched a school reform program to prove what most people would have believed anyway: that students in smaller classes would perform better. Called Project STAR (Student/Teacher Achievement Ratio), the project was conducted over a four-year period in 79 elementary schools across the state. When it was complete, Harvard professor Frederick Mosteller was the man who led the follow-up research team on what he dramatically called "one of the most important educational investigations ever carried out."[1]

The findings of the research were clear: Students who were placed in smaller classes showed significantly higher test scores than those who were not. Ten years later they interviewed the same students (then in tenth grade) and found that they had continued to outperform their peers and also showed "greater initiative with regard to learning activities and less disruptive or inattentive behavior."

In the summer of 1996, encouraged by these long-term results over the past decade, California Governor Pete Wilson led a sweeping reform requiring all California schools to lower the maximum class size from 33 students per teacher to no more than 20 per teacher. It was the largest state education reform in history, projected to cost more than $1.5 billion per year.

The results were mixed. Some academics offered glowing reviews and conclusions similar to those reported by those who looked at the results in Tennessee after the STAR program. Others, including the director of education policy at the American Enterprise Institute, Frederick M. Hess, were not so sure.

The New Stupid

In the 2008/2009 issue of *Educational Leadership* magazine, Hess contributed an article titled "The New Stupid," in which he wrote, "Today's enthusiastic embrace of data has waltzed us directly from a petulant resistance to performance measures to a reflexive and unsophisticated reliance on a few simple metrics. We have pivoted from the 'old stupid' to the 'new stupid.'"[2]

In his article, he proposed three symptoms of this "new stupid":

1. Using data in half-based ways
2. Translating research simplistically
3. Giving short shrift to management data

Turning his attention specifically to the class size reforms in California, he revealed that policymakers made two very obvious blunders. The first was that the mandated class size of 20 in California was still larger than the average class size under the STAR program in Tennessee, which had dictated "no *more* than 20 students." That meant that while many of the Tennessee classes had fewer than 20 students (and therefore an even higher student/teacher ratio), every class in California was *always* the maximum size of 20 students because the state has six times the population of Tennessee.

The second and more serious problem came from the fact that the demographics of California were far different than Tennessee's. Over one third of students in the California school system were "English-language learners" for whom English was not their first language. This made performance in classes, even with smaller students, far more difficult to predict.

These factors made a program that had worked in Tennessee more than a decade before almost impossible to recreate in California. In other words, Hess argued, California had made the most common data mistake you can make: relying on the data without context.

It is a problem that one of the most recognized authorities on data analytics in the world understands as well . . . and has been working to change.

The Sexiness of Analytics

The first time I heard Avinash Kaushlik speak at an event, he nearly got three people fired. He would never have done it on purpose, but I imagine most of his other talks that month had turned out much the same way. Back in 2008, we were both invited to speak at a workshop for about 200 marketing and communications professionals at a large (Fortune 500) technology company. His expertise was web analytics, and mine was marketing, so our presentations were related but different.

Introducing himself as the "analytics evangelist for Google," he took the stage first. Google Analytics is the most commonly used web analytics software on Earth, and the crowd was ready for a dense presentation about charts and numbers. Instead, his first slide featured an image of Angelina Jolie.

"Google Analytics," he shared, "is like Angelina Jolie—undeniably sexy and kicks some major ass." Moving along, he shared terms like "data puking" to describe how we have lots of data that we regurgitate into pages and pages of useless reports, and he talked about unlocking the real power of data to make better business decisions. Then, he got controversial.

Flashing up three screens from our host's website, he proceeded to share all the things that were wrong with them. They weren't optimized, they were collecting the wrong information, and the pages were confusing. With each point he made, you could almost see the web team from the company shrinking lower in their chairs. His ultimate point: *Data alone doesn't tell the whole story*.

"What's missing is the *why*," he notes in his best-selling book *Web Analytics in an Hour a Day*. "Combining the *what* (quantitative) with the *why* (qualitative) can be exponentially powerful."[3] He goes on to make the same point as Hess made with his article: that data alone is meaningless without some way to put it into context. Putting data into context, though, is much easier said than done. One of the main reasons why is because there is so much of it.

Data Overload, Insight Underload

Every activity you do online, from searching for your next holiday destination to purchasing the new best-selling book on Amazon, leaves a series of digital breadcrumbs. These artifacts are data that brands and organizations can and already do use to learn more about you, your habits, what you care about and what types of messages you are most likely to respond to. The data collected on each of us in a single day is unbelievable (and more than a little scary).

It is also just one example of the world of data that businesses have access to . . . and they are not alone. Each of us now has more ways of getting data and statistics into the fabric of our own daily lives, as well. The Nike Plus system has helped runners put sensors in their running shoes to be able to track their runs. Devices like the UP wristband device from Bluetooth headset maker Jawbone and the ZEO Sleep Manager are just two examples of wearable devices that will help you track everything from your health to your sleep patterns.

> **The problem of data overload is that we have no way to extract the meaning from the data in a way that could help us understand what it really means.**

Unfortunately, more data doesn't equal more meaning. In fact, often it can prevent us from garnering any meaning from it at all. So, faced with huge amounts of data and uncertain ways of interpreting what it really means, we do our best. The bad news is that our best can cause a lot of problems.

Four Ways Data Becomes Meaningless

In the never-ending quest to extract meaning from data, people, and organizations end up making the same four common data interpretation mistakes over and over:

1. **Statistical insignificance.** Perhaps the most common mistake in reading any type of data is captured in the ad tagline, "Four out of five dentists recommend this toothpaste." What does that really mean? Did they only ask five dentists? Are they saying that only 80 percent of dentists actually think their toothpaste works? The "data" is insignificant, yet still used to make a specific point.

2. **Wishful extrapolation.** This is the situation that arises when a conclusion from data is based more on wishful thinking than actual data. For example, let's say someone commissioned a research report that asked women to choose between spending an afternoon watching a hockey game or doing their taxes. If 90 percent of women responded that they would rather watch the game, then *wishful extrapolation* would be that 90 percent of women are hockey fans. It only makes sense if you don't think about it.

3. **Inconclusive conclusions.** Sometimes data is inconclusive. That is the problem with doing research and analysis. Yet, a slight leaning one way or another is often used as proof of a certain finding. For example, if 51 percent of hospital clinics have an in-house X-ray machine, the vendor might proudly proclaim that the "majority" of clinics use their machine. Technically, it's true; but it is based on data that is not really that definitive.

4. **Planning paralysis.** The flip side of making conclusions based on inconclusive data is making no choice and being stuck in planning paralysis. Larger companies and those in traditionally risk-averse cultures are often guilty of this. Small decisions take years to make because the pros and cons are endlessly weighed. During that time the subject of the data itself becomes obsolete, making the entire exercise an ongoing cycle of time wastage.

Clearly, we need to get smarter about how we fill in the inevitable gaps that data will create for us. Smart people cannot check their brains at the door when faced with numbers and spreadsheets. We need more meaning.

To find it, many people in business have been referring to the work of a man named Jack J. Phillips . . . without ever realizing it. Though his name may be unfamiliar, the research he did to coin a simple three letter acronym changed the world of business in ways he never expected.

Rethinking ROI

When he invented ROI (Return on Investment) in the mid-1970s, Jack J. Phillips had no idea just how popular it would become. He was working on an idea for his master's thesis in decision sciences at Georgia State University to answer the most fundamental business question of all: *Is the money and time I'm spending doing something actually worth it?* Phillips wanted to create a better answer to that question.

The first glimpse of his emerging solution came in 1973 when he released the world's first impact study for Lockheed-Martin, titled "Measuring the ROI in a Cooperative Education Program." The term *ROI* was officially born. Continuing to hone the idea throughout the 1980s, Dr. Phillips developed his signature ROI Methodology™, "a revolutionary process that provides bottom-line figures and accountability for all types of learning, performance improvement, human resource, technology and public policy programs."[4]

Dr. Phillips' specialty came from helping people within an organization who were running internal programs such as training and internal events to demonstrate the value that their efforts were having on the bottom line of the organization.

In other words, ROI was a concept invented to be able to describe the business value of intangible activities that did not directly sell any products or win any new customers.

Today, the question of ROI is asked in every corner of a business from marketing to customer service. There are even articles online talking about how to calculate your personal ROI. Yet, this search may be clouding our ability to see what really matters, because we are taking a single metric and applying it blindly to everything in our lives without context.

My friend, entrepreneur and best-selling author Gary Vaynerchuk, has a brilliant line he often uses in presentations where he asks the audience to consider this question: "What's the ROI of your mother?" His cleverly stated point is that there are some things that may have intrinsic value even though we typically would never categorize them that way.

ROI, or other hard business metrics that are filled into spreadsheets, are only part of the story. The rest has everything to do with the qualitative side of data—the flip side.

The Flip Side of Data

If data is one side of the decision-making coin, then let's consider observation the flip side. In scientific study, the importance of observation cannot be overstated. It is only through observation that scientists can truly understand what numbers mean and how to explain the nature of the world.

John Hayes, the former CMO of American Express, was famously quoted as saying, "We tend to overvalue the things we can measure and undervalue the things we cannot." In a culture filled with people who demand numbers and research before making any sort of move, those who are able to observe the world around them and take a risk are often the proven winners in any industry.

Many of the most brilliant business decisions in modern history were based on little to no "hard" data—from Steve Jobs deciding that consumers really wanted an iPod to Henry Ford creating his line of Model T automobiles and later declaring that if he had asked consumers what they wanted they would have asked for a faster horse.

This is not to say that data or even good research doesn't matter. Each is important in the right situations. But there is a flip side to data and it has everything to do with emotion and passion and vision and all the sort of things that don't fit neatly onto a spreadsheet. That is the real context you need.

Once you do start paying attention to context, the meaning behind numbers becomes clear.

Why Context Matters (and Your "Sticky" Website Actually Stinks)

Here's a common example: Many companies look at a few standard metrics to understand whether their websites are achieving their purpose. One of the most common is average session time. As the common thinking goes, if you have an average session time of two minutes, that means someone spent two minutes reading all the content on your site. If that time, however, is two *seconds*, then most companies assume their website isn't engaging enough and they start to add features or pay for a costly redesign.

But let's look at this situation in human terms to get more context. Imagine I am a potential customer for a local luggage store, and I want to go into their store for some comparison shopping and potentially to buy a nice new Briggs & Riley bag (my favorite luggage brand). I visit their website and immediately can't find a link to show me their store locations. Assuming that something so obvious must be there somewhere, I click around to a few of the pages on the site looking for an address. After two minutes, completely frustrated, I abandon the site and vow never to go to their store because they didn't have something so obvious in an easy-to-find location—and commit to going elsewhere to buy my bag.

Sound familiar? The irony is that according to the common web metrics, that situation was just recorded by some marketing manager doing a monthly report as a success! In contrast, if I had visited their website, seen an image for a Google map with their address, and clicked on it immediately, I would have spent less than two seconds on their site—and been happily on my way toward their store to spend some real money. This is the problem with relying too much on the quantitative instead of also looking at the qualitative. Perhaps no place allows us to see this more directly than when it comes to politics, as psychologist Drew Westen uncovered in 2008.

The Real Reason Likeable Politicians Always Win

Just over a year before the 2008 U.S. presidential election was getting into full swing, a groundbreaking book on psychology changed the way that people looked at politics. It was called *The Political Brain* by Emory University psychologist Drew Westen, and it took a deep look at why people are influenced to vote the way they do—often when there is considerable evidence to logically sway them in the opposite direction. "In politics, when reason and emotion collide," he wrote, "emotion invariably wins . . . If you want to win voters' hearts and minds, you have to start with the heart, otherwise they aren't going to care much what's on your mind."[5]

His surprising conclusion, which heavily influenced both candidates and their campaigns in 2008, was that *the key is not to appeal to the right or to the left*. Instead, you have to appeal to the electorate as a whole. This conclusion seems on the surface to fly against everything we know when it comes to politics. After all, the political strategists first talk about solidifying your base of voters who will always vote for you and *then* going after the undecided voters.

Trust, as Westen wrote, did not depend on the policies as much as it depended on the individual candidates themselves. For years, the polls on political candidates have measured the qualities of likeability by asking poll respondents to rate the likeability of politicians. Bill Clinton was widely rated more likeable than Bob Dole, and he went on late-night television to play his saxophone to prove it.

George W. Bush, on a personal level, was rated more likeable than the stiff Al Gore during the 2000 election (and before Gore portrayed a more human side of himself in *An Inconvenient Truth*). Voters said they would much rather have a beer with "Dubya" than with Gore (yes, they have a poll that actually asked this question). Barack Obama passed his likeability test in his first election against John McCain in part thanks to a resounding endorsement from Oprah and a televised one-on-one game of basketball with Stuart Scott from ESPN.

> When it comes to matters like deciding who we will vote for, as well as how to interpret data that we are given, emotion is the primary filter that we use.

There is a reason why likeability of candidates has become such a common polling question for years. When it comes to politics, people may say they vote squarely on the "issues," but in reality they often vote based on their emotional connection to the candidates. And whether they show up to vote at all often has everything to do with how likeable a candidate is.

Why Results Matter More than Data

I have never met anyone who wasn't chasing great results. The end goal is the same, whether you are trying to lose some weight or launch a successful startup. The challenge is that we are often so buried in measurable data that we forget to measure *results*.

On a basic level, this is Avinash Kaushlik's mantra that he repeats to organizations every time he teaches them about analytics. It is not about recording what happened. It is about *finding meaning*. When you focus on meaning, you start to realize that the most important thing isn't data or spreadsheets, but results. And results aren't always measured in hard numbers.

For example, in a business context, if you are just focused on the numbers, then generally the most important metric would be sales. Did we increase or decrease sales as a result of this activity? If you can draw a direct line to sales, then whatever you did worked. If you can't, then it didn't. This is the definition of a data-centric approach. It is also the dumbest way to record whether something is working.

Consider these examples:

- For years, the public relations industry used something called Advertising Value Equivalents (AVEs) to measure whether their PR efforts were working. The idea was that you could measure the value of a positive article in a media publication by calculating how much that same space would have cost in advertising dollars if it had been paid for. So a full-page story in the *New York Times* on a product would be the alleged equivalent of $150,000 (or whatever the going rate for a full-page ad happens to be). In 2011, led by Ogilvy Public Relations, the industry finally started moving away from this metric.

- The world of diet and nutrition is filled with meaningless data and measures of health. Calories, for example, are a convenient metric but only tell one small piece of the story. A diet soda has zero calories, but drinking 10 a day will probably lead to long-term health problems. When starting a weight-loss program, many people just focus on reaching a bottom-line number and making their body weigh less. This may work initially if you happen to be obese, but for healthy people, exercising to trade fat for muscle and measuring your BMI (body mass index) is a much better measure.

- If you were in the market to buy a new lawn mower, the first thing you would do is go online and start to narrow your choices (such as deciding between a mower you ride or one you push). Then, you might read some online reviews. During that time, you may read a media article or see a billboard ad. When you are ready to buy, you go to Google, click a text link, and buy the mower. Right now, Google takes credit for the transaction, and helps you to conclude that nothing else mattered. Of course, all of these things worked together to convince you to buy the mower.

So, with all this flawed measurement around us, how can we really get better at understanding what works?

The Five Principles of Likeonomics

Instead of thinking of ways to create a smarter spreadsheet, let's imagine how we might build a more useful framework to understand if the things we are doing are actually worth the effort. That framework is described in the five principles of Likeonomics:

1. Trust
2. Relevance
3. Unselfishness

4. Simplicity
5. Timing

In Part II, we will focus on how these five principles can help you extract more meaning and context from any data, and work together to make you more believable and more trusted.

CHAPTER 3 IN 60 SECONDS
#LIKEABILITYROI #LIKEONOMICS

- Data alone is meaningless without some way to put it in context.
- ROI was first invented to describe the business value of intangible activities that did not directly sell any products or win any new customers.
- Over time, ROI has become overused and rendered meaningless in many situations.
- Thanks to more technology and tools, we are swimming in vast amounts of complex data.
- The problem with this data overload is that it makes it almost impossible to extract meaning.
- Data becomes meaningless in four ways: statistical insignificance, wishful extrapolation, inconclusive conclusions, and planning paralysis.
- We tend to overvalue the things we can measure and undervalue things we cannot.
- When it comes to matters like deciding who we will vote for, as well as how to interpret data that we are given, emotion is the primary filter that we all use.
- We are often so buried in measuring data that we forget to measure results.

   Bottom line: As most of us are swimming in data, we need to find a way to make data more meaningful by focusing on context instead of filling in spreadsheets.

PART II

The Five Principles
of Likeonomics

Truth

The truth is more important than the facts.

—Frank Lloyd Wright

Always tell the truth. That way, you don't have to remember what you said.

—Mark Twain

Phil Donahue didn't know it yet, but his days were numbered. His self-titled *Phil Donahue Show* had been nationally syndicated since 1970, and by 1984 he had risen to become the undisputed king of daytime television, watched by millions every day.

That year, *A.M. Chicago* was the show stuck at a distant second place in the 9 a.m. timeslot that Donahue dominated. With little to risk, they decided to bring in a new and relatively unknown actor and beauty queen with very little experience to anchor the program. No one expected much from her.

In her first few months, she modeled her show's format to be exactly like Donahue. She borrowed her interviewing technique directly from watching Barbara Walters on television. Yet despite her inexperience, audiences responded to her. Early critics were even complimentary, noting that she stood out as "more genuine, and far better attuned [than Donahue] to her audience, if not the world."[1]

Within months, her show took over the number one slot in the regional Chicago local market. In two years her show was nationally syndicated and already competing with *Donahue*. It was a quick start, but looking backward it was only on November 10, 1986, that this up and coming host named Oprah Winfrey would show a glimpse of becoming the legend we now know simply as Oprah.

Oprah's Secret

On that day, the sensitive topic for the show was sexual abuse victims and their molesters. As the show was nearing its end, Oprah stunned her audience by revealing that she had been raped by a relative when she was nine years old. Her deeply personal admission was unlike anything a daytime TV show host had ever shared. At that time, more than 25 years ago, there was a much more distinct separation between personal and celebrity life. Celebrities (and particularly talk show hosts) just didn't reveal that much about themselves. And they didn't have Twitter.

But as Audrey Edwards, the former editor of *Essence* magazine wrote, "By confronting her own worst demons . . . Oprah showed an entire generation of women how to look small and large terrors in the face and beat them down."[2]

It was her extreme honesty that stood out from the first day she went on air, and it was a quality she continued demonstrating for her entire career, as she rose to be one of the most influential women in the world. By the time she went off the air to start her own network in 2011, the media had even given a name to her ability to turn all kinds of products, from books to greeting cards, into bestsellers. They called it the "Oprah Effect."

She had an estimated viewership in the United States of 48 million, and her show was broadcast in 150 countries around the world. Books that were featured as part of her Book Club had sold over 55 million copies collectively. Her endorsement of Barack Obama was widely credited in 2008 with being one of the major factors in his presidential victory. With an estimated net worth of $2.7 billion, *Forbes* recently noted that Oprah is the only female African American billionaire, and ranked her the third-most-powerful woman in the world.[3]

When Donahue retired, he was asked why he thought Oprah had become so popular. "I think she can dish with women better than I can," he said. "She can talk about weight and clothes and men and the real-life drama of a single woman in a more personal way than I can."[4] Not only could she talk about those things in a personal way, but she always did it with the truth.

Are You Building on a Sinkhole?

There is a very good reason why the truth is the first principle of Likeonomics, and it is not hard to explain why. If you were building a house, the worst possible place to build it would be on top of a sinkhole. A favorite natural disaster for writers of fictional medical dramas like *Grey's Anatomy*, sinkholes are real phenomena that happen when the rock under the surface of the ground is made of a material like limestone, which dissolves. Eventually, the surface doesn't have enough support and the entire ground caves in.

Building a business or a personal relationship on a lie is the same as building a house on top of a sinkhole. It may not collapse right away, but eventually something will change and the unstable ground will cave in. The point of starting with the truth is to make sure you're building everything else on safe ground.

Yet, as powerful as the truth can be, it makes sense given the world today to spend a bit of time looking at the other side. If the truth is really a motivator for loyalty and connection, then why do

> In order to be believable, the most successful people and organizations always find a way to share their truth, and then build on it.

so many people and organizations lie so consistently and perfectly? If anyone should be able to answer this, it would be the man affectionately known as "the lie doctor."

The Lie Doctor and the Dalai Lama

Dr. Paul Ekman could be the best liar in the world, if he wanted to be. For the past 30 years, he has been studying lying in all of its forms, from unspoken facial and body movements that indicate deceit to how people behave when they are actually telling lies. He has worked as a clinical psychology officer in the Army, been a consultant for the FBI and CIA, and offered advice to animators at Pixar on facial expressions.

Today, he teaches seminars on "evaluating truthfulness and emotional skills," training everyone from military personnel to business executives. He is also the scientific advisor to a dramatic TV series called

Lie to Me, largely based on his research. Throughout his research, the question that he has studied for decades is: *Why do people lie?*

To answer that, Dr. Ekman notes, the first thing you need to do is ignore little white lies like those in order to be polite (e.g., "that color looks really good on you"). Those are hard to detect, but also usually harmless. Instead, what we should be worried about are what Dr. Ekman calls "serious lies."

In serious lies, there is a threat of significant damage if the lie is discovered: loss of freedom, money, job, relationship, reputation, or even life itself.[5]

Serious lies are at the heart of why we are suffering through the believability crisis, so understanding why they happen is critical. Many of the examples shared in Chapter 1 of unethical behavior from companies or governments were a result of their ability to tell serious lies. In business, it is often easy to see the motivation for lying, because there are short term profits involved. But despite the short term temptation, can people's behavior be changed to behave more ethically? It was a question that even one of the most spiritual men on Earth wanted an answer to.

In March of 2000, an organization called the Mind and Life Institute sponsored a unique gathering of Buddhist monks and behavioral scientists in Dharamsala, India. The meeting was part of a series designed to "foster an exchange between Buddhist tradition and Western science." That year, His Holiness the Dalai Lama participated, and during the meeting he asked the scientists to investigate an important question.

Could the meditation methods that Buddhist monks used help Western audiences avoid "destructive" emotional experiences like lying? Agreeing to explore this question, a team of scientists led by Dr. Ekman and Dr. B. Alan Wallance began a new research study on the topic of "cultivating emotional balance" (CEB).

They conducted their pilot study from September 2002 to May of 2003. Finding a sample group of 15 female schoolteachers, they built a five-week training program that combined lectures and discussions with meditation. After the program, participants were tested and "showed a highly significant decrease in depression, anxiety, and hostility over the five-week period."[6]

So, freeing yourself from hostility and lying can be a good thing for your health, and it can make you happier, too. One of the sad truths we already know about the capitalistic society many of us live in, though, is that emotional well-being might not seem like enough.

Organizations (and many people) want to make money. This is the single biggest reason why the truth is often so hard to openly talk about and share in the modern business world. In fact, there are many forces in the world around us that seem to reward dishonesty, and some of them have real business reasons behind them.

Empowerment versus the Anti-Truth Policy

As much as we would all probably like to be honest people individually, when it comes to organizations there are often well-argued reasons for why the truth may not be something you want to share.

The truth can be buried under the umbrella of *trade secrets* or avoided for fear that competitors might be able to use it to gain some sort of advantage. In a sadly high number of cases, employees are simply not trusted enough to be able to share what they think is right without strict policies. I describe this often as the *Anti-Truth Policy*, and far too many companies have one.

FIVE ELEMENTS OF THE ANTI-TRUTH POLICY

1. **Always Spin** — Focus on the facts instead of the truth behind them.
2. **Embrace Silence** — Don't talk to anyone about anything relating to the company.
3. **No Passion** — Don't ever share your personal opinion on any of our products or services (even if it is glowingly positive).
4. **No Comment** — Don't admit to any wrongdoing or mistakes.
5. **Use Our Legal Sphincter** — Always go through legal as a gatekeeper.

There may be other pieces to this Anti-Truth Policy, which vary from company to company, but the basic elements are usually the same.

It is also the reason why the small handful of companies who manage to put the truth at their core and avoid these types of policies are so celebrated. Both online retailer Zappos and the Four Seasons hotel chain, for example, are known for amazing customer service. Instead of distributing an anti-truth policy, their employees are empowered to do whatever it takes to help a customer.

> **Empowerment is a critical factor in creating a culture of truth because we each need to feel a sense of control over our own actions before we can be comfortable sharing the truth.**

Empowerment of employees and customers was also the topic of years of surveys done by Forrester Research, as well as the main principle explored in the highly useful book *Empowered*, by consultants Josh Bernoff and Ted Schadler.

In it, they demonstrate that people are most engaged when they feel empowered to solve problems and implement their best ideas. And empowerment only happens when you embrace and encourage employees to share the truth.

But what happens when the truth is not so favorable?

Embracing Your Inconvenient Truth

In 1962, Avis Car Rental was a struggling brand that had spent the last 13 years losing money. By the early 1960s, after being in business for nearly two decades, Avis had only managed to earn only a paltry 11 percent of the car rental business in the United States. Their biggest competitor, Hertz, was the market leader by far and Avis was a distant second.

That year, Robert C. Townsend had just taken over as the new CEO and knew he had to act quickly. One of his first acts was to bring in advertising agency DDB and challenge them with a single question: "How do we get 5 million dollars of advertising for 1 million dollars?" The math was based on the simple fact that Hertz was currently outspending Avis five to one on marketing, so Townsend knew his budget would have to work at least five times as effectively.

To develop a strategy, the team from DDB began by interviewing Avis employees. For weeks, they heard the same phrase over and over: "We try harder because we have to." The art director at the time was a man named Helmut Krone who always had a uniquely truthful approach to creating advertising which he once shared in an interview: "It was important to start with a truth about the product and about the company, and create an ad from there, not start with something we had to sell and then figure out what we could come up with."[7]

It was this commitment to the truth that would lead Krone and the DDB team to create one of the most memorable taglines in advertising history: "Avis is only No. 2. We Try Harder." With new visuals and taglines, DDB put the campaign in front of the Avis management team, and everyone had an instant reaction: They all hated it.

What company in their right mind would ever publicly admit in their marketing that they were number two? It felt like admitting to failure before even starting. After all, Olympic athletes don't go for the silver medal. Everyone aims for the number one spot, and you're not supposed to settle for anything less.

As Avis executives soon learned, Townsend had made an agreement with DDB before they started working together. He had ceded control of creative direction and specifically promised that his team would not try to become art directors. He had even distributed an "advertising philosophy" memo to his full team before the ads were presented that forbade them from critiquing the ads on anything other than "a material defect."

In exchange, Townsend demanded that DDB would only present creative ideas that their entire agency was behind and that represented their best thinking. "Don't hire a master to paint you a masterpiece and then assign a roomful of schoolboy-artists to look over his shoulder and suggest improvements,"[8] he preached to his team. It was a unique structure as far as agency-client arrangements went, but together they committed to it and in 1963, the campaign celebrating Avis' position as number two was launched.

Avis told the truth and was even turning it into a competitive advantage. To make sure all the employees at every level knew and believed the new message,

The entire campaign wasn't just honest; it was honest in an unexpected way and that made it memorable.

they all received copies of each print ad in their pay envelopes before it ran. The message was clear: We are number two, and we are okay with it. One of their ads even promised that as a virtue of being number two, "The line at our counter is shorter."

Within a year, the campaign had helped Townsend turn the company around. In 1964, Avis went from losing $3.2 million the previous year to making a profit of $1.2 million. Over the next four years they tripled their market share in the United States from 11 percent in 1962 to 35 percent in 1966. And perhaps the most telling fact of all—more than 40 years later the shortened tagline "We Try Harder" still defines the Avis brand and what it stands for.

Selling Cardboard

Admitting that you are second in your industry may not seem like that difficult of a choice for Avis to make. After all, everyone probably knows it anyway. It might be a slightly counterintuitive marketing strategy, but it's unlikely to send shockwaves through your customers. In the right situation, embracing the truth could even transform your entire business.

In 2009, Domino's Pizza had the perfect storm of bad news. They had conducted focus groups that year where customers described their pizza crust as "cardboard" and said their tomato sauce "tasted like ketchup." Many customers didn't even believe there were real tomatoes in the sauce. The only thing they liked about it, apparently, was the low price and how quickly they could get their ketchup-flavored cardboard delivered. Speed was their top (and perhaps only) priority.

Then, in April of 2009, two rogue Domino's employees filmed themselves doing disgusting things with the pizza they were sending out to customers and posted the video on YouTube. CEO Patrick Doyle apologized, but the damage was already done. Sales of Domino's Pizza started to decline as media reported on the viral video.

The usual marketing solution to a problem like this might be to ride out the storm and then load up on discounts (2 for 1!) or create some new slightly disgusting but somehow irresistible side dish (for Americans) like chocolate-dipped cheese bread with cinnamon.

Doyle, however, decided to tackle this perception problem with an unexpected approach: changing *reality*. The Domino's Pizza team internally was shown the candid feedback from people and challenged to improve their product. They changed everything from the seasoning for the sauce to the ingredients used.

When they finished, the brand ran a new ad about the "Pizza Turnaround," which not only featured customers from real focus groups shown calling the pizza "cardboard," but then put their own team of chefs, marketing executives, and employees in front of the camera to ask them how that made them feel. Then they showed those same customers trying the new and improved pizza, and being pleasantly surprised.

It was real, it was human, and people started to reconsider Domino's. In the first quarter the ads ran, sales increased by double digits. In the United States, same-store sales rose 9.9 percent and in the first quarter of 2011, Domino's announced that the company's net income rose 10.6 percent.

Plenty of companies claim to have a new and improved product. Domino's actually fixed their product, and then offered a glimpse behind the scenes at how and why they did it.

> For customers who were so used to being lied to and manipulated by advertising, to see a company that was telling the truth and admitting their mistakes was a sensation.

People couldn't stop talking about it and responded by buying the product.

Why Being Truthful Is So Hard

Just knowing how much value can come from telling the truth sometimes doesn't make it any easier to do, unfortunately. What holds us back? Usually it is one of the following four reasons:

1. **The truth is ugly, and inconvenient.** What if your product really isn't that good? The most common fear with the truth is that we need to cover it up because it might expose us and our work as being less wonderful than we wish it were.
2. **The truth makes you vulnerable.** As we have seen from the Oprah story, telling the truth can put you into a position of vulnerability. This is a tough thing for anyone to choose to do, especially in a less personal and more public environment.

3. **The truth is hard to see.** Sometimes the real truth can be very hard to uncover. Organizations have long histories with dispersed information. More importantly, many people are used to simply accepting that the truth has been given to them, without digging any further.

4. **The truth can depend on you.** An engineer might look at a product, for example, and see a perfectly usable design, but when that same product is in front of a consumer it becomes an enigma. The truth about that product can differ depending on who you are and how you look at it.

From the rise of Oprah, to Avis embracing their silver medal position in the car rental business, to Domino's admitting their product was bad and fixing it, the truth has many potential ways it can work in your favor. More importantly, as we learned in Part I, there is an urgent need for each of us—and our organizations—to be more believable, and the truth is a critical first step in achieving this.

Still, in having facilitated dozens of meetings and workshops with clients where this question has come up, finding the *right* truth is hard. The truth can be buried. It can feel wrong to share. Sometimes what you uncover may just be a fact and not the underlying core truth at all. So how can you actually find the truth in a way that will be useful?

The Three Elements of Truth

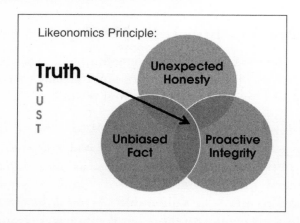

In 2004, two business school professors—James M. Kouzes and Barry Posner—conducted a series of studies that were designed to uncover why anyone would follow a particular leader in what they called "cynical times." As we have seen in Chapter 1, this is a vital question to ask because so many institutions and their leaders still need to earn the trust of their stakeholders.

As part of their research, they asked their participants about the personal values and traits that were most important in a person that they might willingly follow (i.e., take their advice, follow their guidelines, or sign up for their team). "In virtually every survey we conducted," they noted, "honesty was selected more often than any other leadership characteristic."[9]

Every story profiled in this chapter features people and organizations that were able to start with some sort of honesty, but honesty alone is only the first of three elements of truth:

Unexpected Honesty	Unbiased Fact	Proactive Integrity
Honesty offered in an unusual way or on an unexpected topic that will make it more significant.	Something that has actually been done, occurred, or is actually the case, shared in a way that doesn't reveal an inherent bias.	Consistently acting in a way that keeps the promises you have made *proactively* before anyone forces you to.

Domino's act of honestly admitting their pizza tasted awful is unexpected. Oprah honestly revealing intimate personal details about her

> For the truth to stand out, the honesty behind it must be unexpected in some way.

childhood is unexpected. It is the unexpected that separates really powerful honesty from the type of honesty that people expect to see, which is usually described as "transparency." Your goal should be to demonstrate unexpected honesty with the truth, and not simply to aim for being transparent.

Of course, honesty is usually meaningless without an idea of what information you will be sharing honestly. For that reason, you need to have facts. Facts should be the most objective part of the truth, but often they can be the most subjective because of the inherent bias that we all might have toward them.

Any fact can potentially be misused, as we saw in Chapter 3 with the discussion of wishful extrapolation and how data can often be manipulated toward any conclusion. In politics, for example, facts can be a matter of perspective. As politicians and parties try to influence perceptions about their beliefs, facts are often twisted to meet certain ends, or even missing altogether.

Several years ago, the Annenberg Public Policy Center at the University of Pennsylvania created a website called FactCheck.org dedicated to encouraging more real facts as part of the debate. It was desperately needed. With a team of bipartisan reporters, the site investigates claims made by politicians on both sides to see what is true and what isn't.

Unfortunately, there is no magic formula to determine which facts are true or unbiased; but usually you will need to focus on something that is more than just a number.

An unbiased fact is something that goes beyond a result of a survey or report. It is more fundamental than simple data.

The last element is proactive integrity, which is doing what you say you will do. There is plenty of evidence that this is rapidly becoming one of the most important aspects of business. As part of a collective action package, in 2009, Siemens AG partnered with the World Bank to invest $100 million in creating the Siemens Integrity Initiative, which supports organizations and projects that fight corruption and fraud through collective action, education, and training.

One of the initiatives that the partnership is funding with a $3 million grant to the Central European University (CEU) is the creation of a Center for Integrity in Business and Government (CIBG), which will offer education in integrity to business leaders across Central and Eastern Europe. Similar programs are being founded at other universities around the world.

It is when integrity is proactive that it becomes the most powerful demonstration of the character of a person or organization and how much the truth really matters.

The most important lesson any of them will offer is that people and organizations with integrity are the ones that stand beside the decisions they make.

CHAPTER SUMMARY
THREE THINGS TO REMEMBER ABOUT TRUTH

1. Sharing the truth is not the same thing as sharing facts. Truth is something more fundamental and emotional than just a proof point.
2. People respond to human companies in human ways, and sometimes the most human thing you can do is admit an "inconvenient truth," like being number two in your industry or having a product that people hate. When you stand up and tell the truth, and then commit to fixing the problem, it inspires not only likeability, but also loyalty and trust.
3. The most important factor in decision making, ideal for many people—from leaders and from organizations and people they choose to build relationships with—is truth and integrity. Doing business and living life with these principles in mind is no longer a nice thing to have; it is a necessity.

Online Workbook and Action Guide:
How to Be More Truthful

www.likeonomics.com/truth

Relevance

Relevance is the mother of invention.
     —Tim Manners, *Relevance: Making Stuff That Matters*

People don't buy what *you do, they buy* why *you do it. The goal is
to do business with people who believe what you believe.*
     —Simon Sinek, *Start with Why: How Great
     Leaders Inspire Everyone to Take Action*

In 2009, the United Nations decided to host an event that critics predicted would accomplish nothing. The aim was to bring together the world's largest nations to discuss how to collectively address the issue of global warming. The skeptics' concerns were well founded. It was a topic on which the largest nations had never been able to agree. Deciding to move ahead nonetheless, the UN selected Copenhagen as the host location, and the United Nations Climate Change Conference was announced for December of 2009.

A few months before the conference, *TIME Magazine* published a special issue naming a small group of pioneers as "Heroes of the Environment." The list featured many recognizable celebrities and scientists who were well known in the global development community. It was the number one choice in the "Leaders & Visionaries" category; however, that caused a bit of a stir.

His name was Mohamed Nasheed, the newly elected president of the tiny island nation of the Maldives, located in the Indian Ocean off the southern coast of India. Just four months after taking office, he had made headlines around the world for declaring publicly that his government would commit to becoming the world's first fully carbon-neutral nation within 10 years.

A deep concern for the environment was an understandable priority for the Maldives. Of all the places in the world that would be affected by a rise in global sea levels, many experts predicted that the Maldives could be the first due to its low elevation. No single spot in any of the 1,192 islands that make up the Maldives lies more than six feet above sea level. As a result, it is widely thought that what happens to these islands could be a predictor for what will happen to coastal regions across the globe.

Nasheed knew this well when he made his announcement, but he had a big challenge in front of him. As the biggest countries (and polluters) in the world were gathering to speak about an issue that clearly affected his people, how could he ever get enough attention to be part of the debate and have a voice on behalf of his tiny nation of only 400,000 citizens?

Not many people across the world had ever even heard of the Maldives, much less been there. It is by far the smallest nation in Asia, and among the most beautiful, but on a global stage it is nearly invisible. President Nasheed set out to change that.

Two months before the Copenhagen conference, Nasheed summoned his cabinet together and invited them to hold their next meeting completely underwater. Using scuba gear and waterproof paper, the cabinet did exactly that, and they invited the world's media to watch. The underlying message of the stunt was clear. If the world's largest nations couldn't agree on a solution to address climate change, President Nasheed and his people would be the first ones on Earth to be living underwater.

All of a sudden, the environmental movement had a real and powerful visual of what was at stake. If the participating nations did not act, the Maldives was a real country that could be submerged and lost to the world forever. Despite some scientists who claimed that Nasheed was overstating the problem, the stunt worked. It was talked about among participants at the event. It was covered in media across the world.

When it came time to analyze the results from the Copenhagen Summit, they were mixed. Those who celebrated victory pointed to the fact that by January 4th of 2010, 138 countries had signed an agreement to reduce CO_2 emissions. The critics focused on the fact that the agreement was not legally binding and used this to prove that the summit had accomplished nothing.

Perhaps the biggest winner of the entire process, though, was the tiny island nation of the Maldives. As President Nasheed shared with *TIME Magazine*, the rationale for his belief in the relevance of the Maldives to this fight against global warming was clear: "We are on the world's front line. And, in a sense, we are its only hope."[1] Nasheed solved the challenge of relevance for his country, and for at least a moment he put them at the center of what is sure to be one of the most important global media stories of the next decade.

The Relevance Challenge

Sometimes making a big statement is the only way to break through the noise. We often describe things in terms of love and hate, but there is a third and more powerful state that explains how most of us feel when it comes to the vast majority of issues in the world—indifferent. It is impossible to care about everything. Things like irrelevant products and over-the-top sales people are easy to tune out. That is a choice many of us make on an hourly basis without thought.

When it comes to seeing images of people suffering in the world, however, it is harder to ignore. Most of us are personally affected for a short time. Yet, it is a huge challenge for any nonprofit organization to inspire people to *do something* to act on this emotion in a more meaningful way. To illustrate, here is a quick example:

In 2011, the Horn of Africa with parts of Kenya and Somalia were experiencing the worst drought in 60 years. At the time of publication for this book, that drought has continued. Does that bother you? Most of us would, of course, say yes. But if I asked whether you have done anything in the last year to *actually* help people there? Most of us would probably have to say no.

This is not an attempt to make you feel guilty about all the causes you are not supporting, though it might seem like it. Instead, it is an example of why relevance matters so much.

Relevance is not only about getting someone to care about something; it is getting them to care about it RIGHT NOW.

This challenge doesn't just apply to social concerns like poverty or climate change, either. Any of us faces this challenge when confronted with making a new conversation with someone we are meeting for the first time at a party. Managers face this challenge when trying to motivate their workers. Brands face this challenge when trying to convince consumers to consider their products.

As a father *and* a marketer, I can safely say that one of the toughest groups to consistently find some way to be relevant to is also the smallest: my kids. So it is fitting, perhaps, to start the discussion of how to be relevant with the example of a master storyteller—who manages to captivate large audiences of little people who are only united by their size and the fact that they all believe in a man who delivers presents every Christmas from the North Pole.

Canada's Favorite Storyteller

Outside of hockey great Wayne Gretzky, Robert Munsch is the closest thing to a living legend that you are likely to find in Canada. Any parent who has had a child in Canada over the last 30 years probably has a story of their own to tell about reading one of Bob Munsch's stories to their kids when they were younger. A former daycare worker and anthropology student, Munsch actually got his start as a storyteller quite accidentally—as he shares in an entertaining bio on his website:

"Back in daycare I discovered that I could get the kids to shut up during nap time by telling them stories. For 10 years I did this without thinking I had any special skill. After all, while I made the best stories in the daycare centre, most of the other teachers made better Play-Doh."[2]

He only published his first book at the urging of his fellow workers and principal where he worked. It was a story called *Mud Puddle* about a girl named Julie Ann, who is attacked by a mud puddle every time she steps outdoors. It sold just 3,000 copies. He continued writing, though, and each new book did successively better. Most were anything but traditional stories.

In 1980, for example, his story of *The Paperbag Princess* was one of the first to reverse the princess and dragon stereotype by having the princess outsmart the dragon, save herself, and decide *not* to marry the lazy prince because "he was a bum." The book won critical acclaim from feminists and was one of the few children's books to receive an endorsement from the National Organization for Women.

Another thing that set Munsch apart was his aversion to creating a hero character to appear in his books, like Olivia the pig or Corduroy the bear. As he shared on his website, "The first kid I make up the story for sort of 'owns' the story and gets to be the kid in the book—if the story ever gets to be a book." Munsch also had something else besides engaging stories, though, that made him different from the other children's authors of the time.

My wife taught grade school for several years in Ontario, and she remembers how Munsch would often visit local schools and tell these stories in person to children across Canada. His style was silly, animated, and completely mesmerizing for the kids who watched him. As he told his stories, he made funny sounds, jumped around on chairs, and kids quickly learned each story by heart.

These personal connections were what inspired Munsch, as well. Once, while on a book tour in California, he remembers looking at a map and seeing that he was going to be near a school that had written to

Kids loved his stories because they were inspired by real kids, but also because they knew the author personally and could see him perform the stories as he told them.

him. Deciding to visit, he took the letter the class had written, showed it to the school secretary, and said, "Look, Ms. Clebanoff in grade 2 asked me to visit."

These unscheduled stops combined with writing stories that people loved to share helped Munsch become a global success. In 1986, he wrote his best-known book, *I Love You Forever*, a story he wrote as a memorial for two stillborn babies he and his wife had in 1979 and 1980.

The first year of publication, it sold 30,000 copies and was the best-selling kid's book in Canada. The following year, sales doubled. In 1988, it sold one million copies and was also the best-selling kid's book in the United States. In 1994, the *New York Times* updated their list of best-selling children's books and for the first time in years, there was a change in the number one slot. *Goodnight Moon* had officially been replaced by *I Love You Forever*, which has since gone on to sell more than 20 million copies.

Today, Munsch is one of the most beloved storytellers in the world, and his books have been read by millions of children and their parents. What he always understood about relevance was that it would take more than a great story to get kids to care.

Handshakes in Kazakhstan

In the late 1990s, Paolo Nagari was working for a prominent HR training and development firm in Milan. His job sent him to far-flung places across the world, such as Kazakhstan to teach executives skills such as leadership and management skills. As he delivered his workshops, he started to notice something curious. Generally companies would select their highest peformers for international assignments, but not everyone was successful. While some executives who had been relocated to these new regions of the world seemed to be thriving, more than half seemed to be sinking. More interestingly, success did not seem to be based on expertise, motivation, experience, *or* competence.

Are some people or executives just naturally better suited for international roles? It was a question that would consume him for years, until finally one day sitting on his balcony in his adopted home of sunny Charlotte, North Carolina, he started to review years of notes and uncover some interesting patterns.

He began to realize that there were a certain set of traits that made executives thrive. What if he could quantify and start to teach them? That moment led him to develop a core set of teachable principles that he termed "Intercultural Intelligence," a phrase he trademarked. In 2005, he started InterCultural Group, his own consultancy in the United States to teach executives how to succeed in a foreign culture.

At the time, the most popular way to teach executives how to work in new countries was to focus on the do's and don'ts of the culture in question. One of the most popular business books in the world is a thick encyclopedic volume called *Kiss, Bow, or Shake Hands*. It is a country-by-country guide to customs, history, and etiquette designed for business travelers that really popularized this do versus don't approach. Here are a few example tips you might get from flipping through the book:

- In the Philippines, it is expected that people are to be on time for business meetings and late to social events.
- In Brazil, you should avoid scheduling any business activities during the week of Carnival.
- The Turks have a unique way of writing dates, translating December 3, 2010, into 3.12.Thursday.10 (while sometimes the day is eliminated, periods are always used).

What set Paolo Nagari's Intercultural Intelligence® approach apart was that his model does not focus on "dealing" with cultural differences. Most of his competitors were teaching only part of the solution. And he had plenty of evidence in his favor that their approach wasn't working.

According to the most popular statistics on the subject, up to 20 percent of all expatriate assignments end early. Each case costs organizations between $250,000 and $1.2 million depending on factors such as seniority and whether family is involved. In fact, long-term international assignments fail so often that there is even a term to describe the occurrence: *expatriate failure*. It describes not only the premature return home of an expatriate, but also describes the unfortunate fact that their time abroad was probably less than successful.

What was to blame for this extraordinarily high failure rate? Most experts point to the challenge of adjusting to a new culture and communicating effectively as the primary reasons. The simple memorization of a list of things to do might work for a short business trip, but when it comes to making the real adjustments to living in a new culture, this approach is too simplistic.

The first and most critical lesson that Nagari teaches in his course is simple: In order to establish relevance in a new culture, you must focus on the cultural similarities rather than the differences.

His techniques are basic and fundamental ways to help people establish relevance in a new and unfamiliar cultural setting, and they can be learned by any of us. His method shows plenty of

> **Relevance always has to start with an understanding of what the people you want to influence care most about right now, and why they care about it.**

signs that it may be the right way to go, as he has trained executives in a dozen countries for companies like Google, Electrolux, and GE Healthcare.

His participants have dramatically better results from their travel, and an average of 98 percent report that they are highly satisfied with the seminar and likely to recommend it to a colleague. His main insight is the same today as it was when he started: People need to see the world from another point of view and focus on similarities instead of "dealing" with cultural differences.

In part, it is also why staying relevant is so easy for large organizations to forget as they start to focus inward on themselves. This inward focus also describes perfectly the situation the World Bank was facing back in 1994, a year that should have been a fiftieth anniversary celebration for the Bank, but wasn't turning out to be much of a celebration at all.

The Renaissance Banker

The World Bank is one of the largest organizations in the world dedicated to the challenge of ending poverty globally. The early 1990s, however, had been tough years for the Bank.

In 1991, an independent review on the quality of the Bank's projects had concluded, "The proportion of unsatisfactory projects had increased from 11 percent in the early 1980s to 37.5 percent for projects completed in 1991." The Bank itself was suffering from its reputation as a bureaucratic mess.

Some changes had to be made, and chief among them was finding a new leader. The man who would eventually get the job, James D. Wolfensohn, had been waiting for the call for almost 15 years.

Before he was appointed to lead the World Bank, Wolfensohn had been many other things outside his day job as an investment banker. In his youth, he competed for his native Australia as a fencer during the 1956 Summer Olympic Games in Melbourne. He was an officer in the Royal Australian Air Force. He had performed as a concert cellist at Carnegie Hall, and been a chairman of both Carnegie Hall and the John F. Kennedy Center for the Performing Arts.

When he was selected by then U.S. president Bill Clinton as president of the World Bank, Wolfensohn's victory was widely credited to his likeable personality, personal charm, and the time he had taken over the previous years to make sure that despite his varied resume, he still managed to have enough relevant experience for the job.

As Wolfensohn's biographer and *Washington Post* columnist Sebastian Mallaby described, the moment he was appointed The World's Banker, "not only did the Europeans and shareholders acquiesce to the American choice, they seemed positively thrilled by it . . . each [of the directors] had a story about Wolfensohn; he was known to some because of some act of philanthropy, some banking tour de force, or some appreciated cultural gesture."[3] Mallaby described him fittingly as "the Renaissance president."

Making the Bank Relevant Again

Winning the leadership, though, and actually leading were two different things. When Wolfensohn took over, the average project at the Bank took two years to prepare, and the internal processes were labored, multi-tiered, and complicated.

Wolfensohn had come from the private sector and worked with financial institutions like Citigroup and Solomon brothers where deals were often made based on handshakes, and personal relationships were at the heart of nearly every decision. As a result, his natural inclination was that the Bank needed to do more listening to build relationships with the people in third-world, poverty-stricken nations that they were trying to help.

In 1998, inspired by a study called *Assessing Aid*, which concluded that "putting people in developing countries in control was indeed the key to more successful projects," Wolfensohn would make a bold change to the Bank. It was a move that would also affect my own life in an unexpected way.

Everyone Who Matters Knows *You*

In 1995, the World Bank policy was to have every one of their country directors who led Bank projects for a particular country or region based in Washington, DC. Wolfensohn thought these managers should be based in the local countries where the projects were being done instead of remotely in Washington. Over the next several years, he would steadily move dozens of top managers within the Bank to manage country offices by living in various countries around the world.

Two years later, after having worked at the Bank for nearly 25 years, my father agreed to become one of these country directors and accepted the job of managing the Philippines office. When Dr. Vinay Bhargava first took over as country director of the Philippines, it was the first time that the Bank had committed someone directly to the country to oversee the impact of all the Bank-funded projects and represent the Bank to the local media, civil society, private business, and government.

It was not an easy assignment. Up until that point in the Philippines, the Bank had mostly talked only to the government and suffered from the legacy of its support for ousted Filipino leader Ferdinand Marcos. Naturally, people were skeptical. To build trust, my father had to demonstrate that the Bank was invested in the people of the Philippines and not just the government. The biggest challenge would be to build relationships, earn the Filipinos' trust, and make the Bank likeable.

Wolfensohn, for his part, was adamant that all of his country directors use the same kind of relationship building that he had counted on to get his dream job in the first place.

> **The fundamental idea was to build relationships, with a slight twist. It wasn't just about who you knew; it was important that everyone knew *you* and believed that you cared.**

He believed that through these personal relationships of individuals, the entire Bank could be involved in the daily political, NGO, and business sector work in each region, and thereby become a stronger partner of the local economies to help create prosperity and fight against poverty, hunger, and other social issues.

So for the next five years, my parents' home would become a venue for entertaining. They would attend government functions and parties (which the Filipinos were particularly fond of throwing). And my father would build relationships that would last for more than a decade. This huge investment in relationship building by Wolfensohn on a global scale and by my father in the Philippines started to pay off.

People began to rethink how they saw the World Bank. International groups protesting the mission of the Bank started to turn their activism into dialogue with the Bank. People started to have more pride in working at the World Bank. And in the Philippines, the Bank became the largest global lending institution and one of the most trusted partners of the government *and* the people in the country.

The Philippines was not the only success story either. Mallaby credited the decentralized move of country directors to the field with helping to create a "humbler, less hectoring vision of the Bank" and called it Wolfensohn's "chief managerial achievement."[4] By 2005, when Wolfensohn stepped down as president after two terms, 71 percent of country directors were based outside of Washington, DC, in countries around the world, and the Bank enjoyed a much closer relationship with all the countries it was serving. Wolfensohn's legacy is described on the World Bank web site as "the 'Renaissance Banker' [who] pushed through reforms that have made the Bank more inclusive."

Why Is Relevance So Hard?

Whether your audience is children, international business travelers, or local politicians and nonprofits, the challenge of relevance can be difficult. And this is not only because getting people to care is generally difficult. There are a few other reasons why real relevance can be so hard to achieve:

1. **Relevance is easy to assume.** When you think about answering the question of whether you are sharing something that is relevant, it is easy to assume that the default response would be yes. After all, if you sell bikes and you know that someone searched for a bike store on Google, you know that bikes are relevant to them. They just searched for the word, right? The important thing to remember is just because a topic is relevant for someone *doesn't mean that you automatically have relevance to that topic.*
2. **Relevance requires you to know your audience.** Unlike a principle such as truth, which can be seen as something of an absolute,

relevance can be different for different people. As a result, offering something that is truly meaningful often requires the extra step of really understanding the people you will be talking to.

3. **Relevance can be tough to scale.** When you have a principle that can change based upon whom you are talking to, you can't necessarily count on the same thing to make something relevant to a wide group of people. When it comes to considering how you interact with multiple groups of people, this might lead you to share something differently from conversation to conversation.

People care about other people and the relationships they build. The best way to combat these barriers is to first find a way to be personally relevant to people around you, and then build the right relationships.

The Three Elements of Relevance

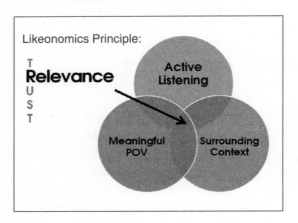

Julian Treasure is an expert in psychoacoustic theory and one of the leading experts in the world in how sound affects business. Aside from his consulting business, Treasure is also a noted speaker on the impact of sound and listening in our lives.

In a TED presentation in 2011, he shared that the greatest problem facing the world right now may be what he calls our loss of "conscious listening," where we truly pay attention to what is happening around us. It is an insight similar to what drives Paolo Nagari to teach executives how to relate to different cultures by seeing the similarities instead of the differences.

Active Listening	Meaningful Point of View	Surrounding Context
Paying attention to the world around you in order to identify the right opportunities where people might care about you and what you have to share.	Having something useful to say or do that adds value to a particular situation or someone's life.	The situation surrounding an event or object makes a big difference in how we perceive it, and whether it will matter to us or not.

Listening cannot just be a passive activity, though. When James Wolfensohn was looking to make an impact at the Bank, he had to

Relevance has to start with understanding, and understanding always starts with listening.

look outward and pay attention to how the Bank was perceived by others before he could act. For Mohamed Nasheed, it was only by paying attention to greater world events that he could find the right opportunity to make his country relevant on a world stage. The first element, therefore, involves an ongoing dedication to more active listening.

Once you have built some level of understanding about the situation and perceptions around you, offering a meaningful point of view is critical. One of the hottest topics in the business world today that will continue to grow is the importance of content in communications. People use terms like _content marketing_ and _curation_ to describe this concept in various ways.

Fashion brand Louis Vuitton, for example, has a "luxury storytelling" website called NOWNESS, where they collaborate with designers and thinkers to tell stories

The main idea is that all forms of communications actually work better when you have something meaningful to say.

influencing contemporary culture and global lifestyle.

What multiple companies have realized is that having a meaningful point of view is a necessity to make your organization relevant to your customer and the world. Nothing makes a message fade into the noise more easily than if you are saying the same thing that countless people have said before and offering it without a considered point of view. When you do have something to say, people are much more likely to pay attention, particularly if it is useful or helps them to solve a problem or think about an issue in a new way.

The final element to relevance is making sure to have the right context. To understand the power of having the right context, the simplest place to look is at the psychological principle known as the *Context Effect*. A classic example of this effect is below:

THE CAT

Most of us would have no problem reading this as *THE CAT* even though technically the *H* and the *A* are identical. In the absence of information, our minds are hardwired to fill in the required context in order to get meaning and find relevance.

The study of archaeology offers another example of the importance of context. Today, most archaeologists use a recording system created back in 1976 for recording all the context around any artifact found, from the place to the type of soil and layers. When a site is properly excavated, you can learn everything about a culture and people. The context makes the difference for an archaeologist, and without it almost any artifact would be meaningless.

It is the perfect analogy for the importance of relevance in everything that we do. Without it, our actions and the things we say simply don't matter enough for anyone to care.

CHAPTER SUMMARY
THREE THINGS TO REMEMBER ABOUT RELEVANCE

1. Relevance is constantly shifting. The most important thing to remember about relevance is that it not just about getting people to care about something; it is getting them to care about it right now — so they can eventually be inspired to *do something*.

2. Without some insight into what the people you want to influence care about, it will be impossible to find a way to be relevant. For that reason, relevance always has to start with some sort of active listening or way to build understanding.
3. The most powerful relevance comes from combining a meaningful point of view and having something to say with the right context for it to really matter.

Online Workbook and Action Guide:
How to Be More Relevant

www.likeonomics.com/relevance

Unselfishness

We have always known that heedless self-interest was bad morals; we know now that it is bad economics.

—Franklin Delano Roosevelt

There are many things that we would throw away if we were not afraid that others might pick them up.

—Oscar Wilde

Almost exactly two weeks after Steve Jobs passed away in October of 2011, Apple held an invitation-only event to celebrate his life. One of the most powerful moments of the event was the heartfelt remarks of Jony Ive, Apple's chief designer and long-time collaborator with Jobs. In his eulogy speech at Jobs memorial service, he shared what he felt made Jobs so different:

> *I think he better than anyone understood that while ideas ultimately can be so powerful, they begin as fragile, barely formed thoughts, so easily missed, so easily compromised, so easily just squished.*

It was a powerful reminder of the fragility of great ideas. It would also have been a fitting eulogy for another business legend named Robyn Putter who had passed away just a year earlier. Born in 1950, Putter had risen through the ranks of the marketing world in his native South Africa after joining global agency Ogilvy & Mather in 1976.

Eventually taking the reins at Ogilvy South Africa as CEO, he built his regional office into a global powerhouse that managed to become the first African agency ever to win the coveted International Agency of the Year award from *Advertising Age* magazine in 1995. When he tragically lost his battle with cancer in March of 2010, worldwide Ogilvy Chairman Shelly Lazarus honored him by sharing that "beyond David Ogilvy, there are few people who have made a greater contribution to Ogilvy's creative reputation."[1]

One of the most powerful ideas he left behind, though, would come from a single conversation in 2006 with brand planners Colin Mitchell and John Shaw, where he made the simple observation (see box).

> **"The brands we most admire are built not just on big ideas, but on big ideals."**

Creating an Ideal World

That fragile idea inspired Mitchell and Shaw to launch an ambitious research project. The premise was simple: brands that have stronger ideals will do better in the long run. In our world of what author Simon Mainwaring has called "me-first consumerism," this might instantly seem like a hard thing to prove. After all, in Chapter 1, we saw how entire social movements have started mainly against companies who seem to put profit ahead of anything else.

The financial and insurance sectors have been the most common targets of consumer rage, but the examples of companies who have focused on short-term results as a priority is lengthy—thanks largely to the fact that publicly traded companies are required to report results quarterly. Even Apple is not immune to criticism thanks to their strategic refusal to make products affordable and their reluctance to share secret details about the working conditions or environmental impact of their manufacturing process.

Yet Mitchell, Shaw, and the rest of the Ogilvy team also had plenty of anecdotal evidence to support the idea that ideals matter for success. Working with dozens of the world's largest brands in a global marketing agency gave them both a credible vantage point to look at what worked and what didn't in business. But what did the *big ideaL* actually mean?

What makes a good big ideaL?

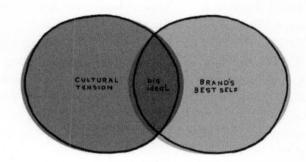

Over four years, they led teams to conduct research to investigate the theory. They interviewed clients and spoke with industry analysts. Ultimately they learned that having a big ideaL came down to two parts. The first required understanding the *cultural tension* of the world at that point. This was the world within which the brand had to be relevant and meaningful. The second part was what the team dubbed the *brand's best self* and represented an aspirational statement of what the brand would like to be. The big ideaL was the intersection.

But simply defining the big ideaL wasn't enough. If they were going to bring it to real clients, it needed more real proof. To accomplish this they commissioned a study in 2009 to conduct interviews with over 2,000 consumers across the United States, the United Kingdom, Russia, China, India, Brazil, Spain, and Germany. The results were encouraging. It showed that brands with stronger big ideals outperformed the lowest rated brands by 2.8 times.[2]

Going further, the study profiled the example of the Shangri-La Hotel brand, which had struggled to stand out in an Asian market where luxury business hotels all focused on treating their customers like kings. Thinking through the big ideaL, their key insight was simple: "It isn't the chandeliers that bring guests back, it's the people. Shangri-La has a culture of treating guests like family—as kin, not king."[3]

That nuance made all the difference. The mission energized employees and reminded them that the human warmth of how they treated guests was most important—*not* putting them on a pedestal as you might for royalty. Once they realized this unique point of differentiation, their marketing communicated it and their team delivered it.

The impact on sales was immediate. Occupancy increased by almost four times the industry average. Revenue did even better, growing 24 percent versus the industry average of 6 percent. And the experience of the Shangri-La brand was not an isolated incident.

Since 2007, the Ethisphere Institute has been producing rankings of the *World's Most Ethical Companies.* In 2011, they released their fifth year of rankings, and more companies than ever before had made the list. They also found that the gap between companies categorized as "ethical" and those listed on the S&P 500 was increasing each year. By 2011, ethical companies were outperforming those listed on the S&P 500 by over 30 percent (see Figure 6.1).[4]

The conclusion of the report stated definitively that ethical companies do have a consistent edge when it comes to being more profitable.

Clearly, there is a real value for brands in choosing to focus on making an impact on society beyond profits. Whole Foods, Patagonia, TOMS Shoes, Starbucks, and

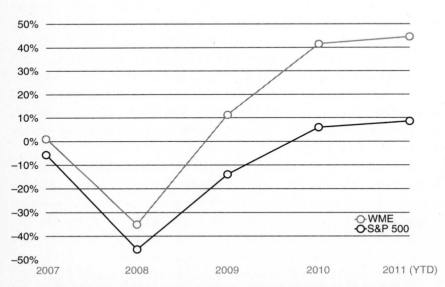

Figure 6.1   Percent Returns—World's Most Ethical Companies versus S&P 500

Source: Ethisphere

Timberland are just a few of the brands that are often profiled as being among the most unselfish and ethical organizations in the world. Every year, as the Ethisphere Institute found, more brands devote their missions to operating in an ethical way.

At Ogilvy, the big ideaL is still the agency's philosophy on how brands can thrive. It is taught to new brand planners and senior leadership alike across the Ogilvy network and its 450+ offices around the world. It remains an idealistic *and* proven view of how companies can do business in ethical ways and make money at the same time. It is also the philosophy that has propelled one of the most beloved retailers in the world to more than a decade of success.

The Ethical Warehouse

The biggest clue that Jim Sinegal was not your ordinary CEO came in an article in *The Seattle Times* a few months before his retirement. The headline read: "Jim Sinegal takes pay cut in last year as Costco CEO." If that seems like an extraordinary thing for a CEO to do, it's not all that makes Sinegal and the members-only warehouse retailer Costco unique.

Costco has a rule that no branded items can be marked up more than 14 percent and no private-label brand item more than 15 percent. In contrast, some of their competitors markup as much as 50 percent for products such as fashion items. The policy comes directly from Sinegal's belief that the path to building a successful company is passing savings directly to customers. He is fanatical about it.

As Costco fresh food buyer Jeff Lyons once explained, the store managers used to dread the monthly budget meetings with Sinegal for a single reason: "Our margin goal is 10 percent, and there'd better be a very good reason you did better than that. Otherwise Jim will say, 'Well, why didn't you lower prices?'"[5]

As if a CEO taking a pay cut and a limit on profits wasn't enough, Costco has also built a reputation as one of the most generous employers in the retail sector. Their standard employee salary of $17 per hour is more than two times the federally mandated U.S. minimum wage and nearly 50 percent more than their closest rival. In addition, the full health and 401(k) benefits are perks that have helped Costco maintain an extremely low employee turnover and low theft rates (a common issue for other retailers).

You might be tempted to think that with all this generosity toward employees and customers, Costco would be lucky to break even. They are certainly no darling on Wall Street, as Deutsche Bank analyst Bill Dreher once complained, "Costco continues to be a company that is better at serving the club member and employee than the shareholder."

Sinegal, though, takes this type of criticism from money-hungry Wall Street analysts in stride. "We think when you take care of your customer and your employees, your shareholders are going to be rewarded in the long run. And I'm one of them [shareholders]; I care about the stock price. But we're not going to do something for the sake of one quarter that's going to destroy the fabric of our company and what we stand for."[6]

So far, the philosophy is working. Since its founding in 1983, Costco has grown at about 15 percent every year with $88.9 billion in revenue for 2010. They are the biggest seller in the United States of fine wines and the average Costco store generates nearly double the revenue of an average store from their closest competitor, Sam's Club.

It is an impressive result for a company described by the media as the "Anti-Wal-Mart," as they refuse to charge their customers more or shave the benefits and salary of their employees. Yet, as Sinegal (who is retiring in 2012) is painfully aware, Costco seems to stand alone in their unselfish behavior. Why don't more companies adopt this approach to business if it works so well?

One popular argument why they don't is the view that businesses (and people by extension) are inherently selfish. There is a wide body of research and thinking to support the argument that at a basic level, people always focus on themselves first thanks to the natural human instinct for self-preservation.

What about the Selfish Gene?

In 1976, an evolutionary biologist named Richard Dawkins wrote a book called *The Selfish Gene*. In it, he elaborated on his research that suggested people were genetically predisposed toward a sort of "social Darwinism" in which we each would look out for ourselves first. His theories were centered on looking at people through the lens of a biologist. As a result, his theories predicted that there may be selfish behavior in nature out of necessity, but the alternative was also true. He would go on to write that this idea also explained what you might call "biological altruism"—the instance that explains moments like when bees commit suicide using their stingers to protect the hive.

Author Mary Midgley posited another theory in her book *Evolution as Religion*, saying, "People not only are selfish and greedy, they hold psychological and philosophical theories which tell them they ought to be selfish and greedy."[7]

All of these were shades of the theory that author Ayn Rand also popularized by calling "rational egoism," or rational selfishness. Her philosophy was that any action was rational if it maximized one's self interest. In 1964, she published a book on the topic called *The Virtue of Selfishness*, where she argued that one's own happiness should be the highest purpose in life.

For decades, this argument persisted. In 2000, Robert D. Putnam delivered what should have been the knockout blow in favor of the selfishness argument. His book *Bowling Alone* profiled what he called the collapse of community, where large groups of people "began to join less, trust less, give less, vote less, and schmooze less."[8] The cover of his book featured the powerful image of a man bowling alone, a sport that Putnam noted only five years earlier was usually done with others and seen as a social activity.

But that same year something fundamental had started to change. The dot-com boom was just beginning, and the Internet was offering a way for people to connect with others around the world. The Internet didn't change people overnight into more selfless and altruistic people. It hasn't really done it over the long term either. But it was one of several factors that started to expose that perhaps we aren't quite as selfish as some thinkers and scientists have made us out to be.

Wikinomics and the Rise of Collaboration

The first time I read *Wikinomics* by Don Tapscott and Anthony D. Williams, I expected the opening story might be about the rise of Wikipedia. On any level, it is the most significant global example of the power of unselfish collaboration, with millions of editors and over

4 million content pages created without any financial compensation. Instead, they told the story of Goldcorp, a traditional gold mining business that realized great success in March of 2000 by issuing their "GoldCorp Challenge," where prize money was offered to anyone who could help GoldCorp calculate the best places to dig for gold in one of their mines.

Their biggest risk was to share all of their proprietary data about mining sites online and invite anyone to contribute—a move that was unheard of in their closed and secretive industry. Suggestions for digging locations came in from around the globe, and more than half were for dig locations that GoldCorp themselves had *not* identified. Much to their surprise, more than 80 percent of those suggested locations resulted in "substantial quantities of gold."[9]

As Tapscott and Williams went on to conclude, the Internet has allowed some of the most fruitful collaborations in modern history, even more significant than digging up lots of gold. From scientists working together to map the human genome to new open source programming platforms like Linux—the positive examples of unselfish collaboration are all around us.

> **The power of mass collaboration goes far beyond just Wikipedia.**

In some cases, like the GoldCorp Challenge, people may contribute for the promise of a reward. But in many cases, they are simply sharing their expertise and passion online because they want to be a part of something.

Finding the Altruism Gene

Why do people contribute to a group effort when there is no promise of financial reward or duty to participate? Why do they choose to help others without expecting anything in return? Collaboration is one of the most popular topics for scientists who focus on human behavior. And it is often one of the biggest enigmas.

In late 2010, researchers at the University of Bonn in Germany claimed to have discovered the "altruism gene." Their research showed that certain people who gave more to charity tended to have more dopamine, the neurotransmitter associated with positive emotions, released into their brain when doing something altruistic. Of the people who might possess one of two elements they tagged as altruism genes, they also learned that roughly 75 percent of all people have one or the other.

In August of 2011, a Harvard law professor named Yochai Benkler went further to describe the effect of this unselfish gene as an overarching human quality that all of us have to some degree. "Through the work of hundreds of scientists," Professor Benkler writes, "we have begun to see mounting evidence in psychology, organizational sociology, political science, experimental economics, and elsewhere that people are in fact more cooperative and selfless, or at least behave far less selfishly, than most economists and others previously assumed."[10]

The most comprehensive look at why altruism works may come from a pioneering new research center in California. Inspired by a visit from His Holiness the Dalai Lama to Stanford in 2005, neurosurgeon and entrepreneur Dr. James Doty founded the Center for Compassion and Altruism Research and Education at Stanford University. The mission of the center is to conduct "rigorous scientific studies of compassion and altruistic behavior."

Uncovering the reasons and motivations for people and organizations that behave in an unselfish way is an important pursuit to help us understand the world around us. If we truly understood this, we might be able to build more incentives for people to behave in more unselfish ways. Perhaps no industry sits at the heart of this opportunity more squarely than health care, where the issue of compassion and altruism intersects everyday with the harsher reality of the economics of medicine.

When it comes to getting medical treatment, how should we balance the necessary importance of technical skills with the ideal of delivering compassionate care? There is a fierce debate already under way to try and answer this question.

Do Doctors Need to Be Competent *and* Kind?

In late 2011, Dr. Lisa Rosenbaum was worried about the state of her profession. As a highly respected physician and an editorial fellow at *The*

New England Journal of Medicine, what she had been reading about in the media was disturbing her intensely.

Driven to share her frustration, she wrote an editorial that was published in the *New York Times* titled "The Downside of Doctors Who Feel Your Pain," where she proposed a single question: "Will our quest to eradicate the coldhearted physician know-it-all be another fad with consequences we may later regret?"[11]

The quest she was referring to is a growing trend within the medical community to focus on educating medical students more deeply on how to have effective doctor-patient relationships. As anyone who has visited with a doctor who was too abrupt or unwilling to listen knows, this relationship hasn't always been the most positive.

> Too often, doctors are seen by patients as arrogant or too busy to take enough time to explain procedures and efforts, or to demonstrate enough empathy.

This was the experience that a woman named Carolyn Bucksbaum had decades ago at a hospital with a physician who dismissed her intuition about having a particular condition and did not listen to her. Ultimately, it turned out that she was right.

Years later, when visiting the University of Chicago Medical Center, she received a completely different type of treatment from a doctor named Mark Siegler. She was so impressed with the experience that she and her husband decided to donate $42 million to the hospital for the creation of a new institute called The Bucksbaum Institute for Clinical Excellence (which is, in itself, an example of Likeonomics at work!).

The main aim of the new Institute is to educate medical students on how to have better doctor-patient relationships. Dr. Seigler describes it as "an ambitious effort to put compassion and empathy on the same pedestal as science and technology."[12] For Dr. Rosenbaum, the Institute was the biggest example of what she saw as a trend toward discounting the importance of real clinical treatment expertise for the "softer" skills of better patient interaction. There were plenty of other doctors who agreed with her. The question Dr. Rosenbaum wrote about in her critical *New York Times* piece was whether this might end up excluding "the awkward student in the corner who obsessively follows a checklist" in favor of "his charming friend who lights up the room."

Why People Don't Sue Likeable Doctors

There is plenty of evidence to suggest that preparing every doctor as if he or she were meant to have a solitary career as a researcher rarely inter- acting with patients doesn't work. One example comes from Malcolm Gladwell, who writes in his book *Blink*:

> *The risk of being sued for malpractice has very little to do with how many mistakes a doctor makes. Patients don't file lawsuits because they've been harmed by shoddy medical care. Patients file lawsuits because they've been harmed by shoddy medical care—and something else happens to them.*[13]

Alice Burkin, a leading malpractice lawyer he interviews, shares this observation: "People just don't sue doctors they like." In fact, when pressed to consider suing a doctor who may be at fault based on the facts of their case, Burkin says they will often reply, "I don't care what she did. I love her, and I'm not suing her."

Of course, just in case not every patient is so willing to forgive, the simplest solution is to try and avoid mistakes. Certainly more education and a stronger adherence to following procedure might help. Surgeon and Harvard Medical School professor Atul Gawande argues for how checklists might help to accomplish this in his groundbreaking book *The Checklist Manifesto*. Yet, even taking these actions is unlikely to remove mistakes completely—after all, doctors are still human.

A Harvard School of Public Health report published in 2003, for example, estimated that physicians reported less than 30 percent of their mistakes. It went on to say that 44 percent of specialists claimed they were actively discouraged from reporting mistakes. Medicine is far from an exact science.

Mistakes, however, are still a relatively rare occurrence among the millions of interactions and treatment that medical professionals offer to patients around the world every day. There will always be a chance that treatments don't work, even when administered correctly. Sometimes, patients die or experience unexpected results, and there is little you can do about it. There is, however, a critical factor in treatment that has little to do with *what* you do and everything to do with *how long you take to explain it.*

In the mid-1990s, two independent studies conducted in Canada and the United Kingdom simultaneously uncovered almost identical conclusions about why doctor–patient interactions matter so much. In the first, University of Toronto researcher Dr. Wendy Levinson found that doctors who had never been sued spent more than three minutes longer with each patient than those who had been sued. She also learned that they were more likely to laugh, engage in more active listening, and make "orienting comments"[14] such as "first we will do this, then we will do that."

The second study conducted by researchers in the Department of Psychiatry at St. Mary's Hospital in London found that the "decision to take legal action was determined not only by the original injury, but also by insensitive handling and poor communication after the original incident."[15]

Clearly, kinder and gentler doctors don't get sued as often, but what about when it comes to patient outcomes? Researchers have been able to show repeatedly that patients who have strong relationships with their doctors are more likely to follow prescribed health activities, as well as be more honest and upfront when discussing their health (which can aid doctors in making earlier diagnoses of all kinds of conditions).

> **Put simply, the more time a doctor is able to spend with her patients, the more likely they are to be healthier, get diagnosed with any condition earlier, and adhere to any prescribed drugs or activities.**

The only remaining barrier is the potential cost, because taking more time with each patient can cost money and doctors are not always compensated for the extra time it takes to provide a more positive bedside manner. Back in 1997, William G. Pickering addressed this argument in an article in the *Journal of Medical Ethics* in which he wrote, "Just as rudeness, indifference, or tactlessness can be achieved in an instant, so can kindness. Indeed, the transmission of sensibility can often take less time than the writing of a prescription."[16]

Thanks to initiatives like the Bucksbaum Institute, there are other forces helping to break down this incentive and time barrier, as well. For example, just a few weeks after the Institute was first announced, the U.S. Centers for Medicare & Medicaid Services (CMS) promised to collaborate with private payers to reward physicians for engaging better with patients and being more available to them.[17]

There are few industries where anyone could argue that compassion matters more than in medicine. Focusing on improving the doctor-patient relationships will continue to be important. Aside from helping to reduce lawsuits, there is growing evidence that more unselfishness from doctors as part of treatment can actually also improve health outcomes.

How the Unselfish and Compassionate Will Rule the World

Derek Coburn is another believer in the power of unselfishness. As a financial advisor, he used to bring his clients together frequently to host networking lunches, but after doing them for several months he noticed something surprising. People who were making great business connections during lunch ended up never following up with one another. So one night he sent 35 e-mails to connect people together after one of his lunches. Fifteen ended up meeting, and five did deals to start working together.

Inspired by the success, he and his wife, Melanie, created their own networking group, which they called CADRE (Connecting Advocates, Deepening Relationships, Exclusively). Attending one of CADRE's lunches is an experience in *un-networking*. In traditional networking, you are focused on selling yourself in a quick elevator pitch. At CADRE, the first question anyone asks is "How can I help you?"

The exclusive, invite-only group pulls people from every industry imaginable and unites them by philosophy. Each member commits to focusing not on themselves and their business, but on helping other members of the group make valuable and meaningful connections. In less than a year, the community has grown to more than 100 members.

There are plenty of other examples in the growing world of the web that unselfishness is a fundamental behavior people can't help watching and sharing online:

- In December of 2010, Yahoo! launched a new social experiment they called "How Good Grows." It was centered on a website (kindness.yahoo.com) where people could post tweets and Facebook status updates of good deeds they were doing with the hope that they could inspire others to do the same and spread that inspiration through social networks online. As part of the project, Yahoo! selected "10 Inspiring Acts" of extraordinary people doing kind things that were spreading to people around the world. In one story, a girl named Caitlin Boyle decided to start a movement called "Operation Beautiful," where women could write inspirational messages to one another on Post-it notes and share them in unexpected locations. The project inspired hundreds of thousands of messages and spread to every continent but Antarctica.
- Another famous global example of online unselfishness is the Free Hugs campaign started in 2004 in Sydney, Australia, by a man who goes by the pseudonym "Juan Mann." Holding up a cardboard sign advertising FREE HUGS, his social movement was profiled in a YouTube video posted in 2006, which has since been watched more than 71 million times.

To find unselfishness in a personal context can be a powerful thing. When it applies to an entire culture, as it has in Japan, you can find some amazing examples of what people are willing to do for one another, even in the face of an unimaginable tragedy.

How Japanese Citizens Responded to Disaster with Unselfishness

Almost a month after a devastating earthquake and tsunami ripped through the Tohoku region of Japan in March of 2011, the *Japan Times* newspaper wrote an article that would create worldwide disbelief. Local Japanese citizens who had lost everything were combing through the rubble to find their belongings. Amidst the mess, those citizens found cash. In fact, they found tens of millions of yen in cash, which most likely would never be able to be traced back to its original owners. It would have been easy to keep. It would even have been understandable. But it was being returned to the government by the millions. What would cause people to display this extreme sort of honesty?

In the story, a man named Shigeko Sasaki was interviewed and shared, "I want anybody picking up money to donate it to disaster-hit areas instead of keeping it for themselves." Japanese law did allow anyone who returned money to keep it if it remained unclaimed after 90 days, so there was some motivation to return it, but the majority of people did not seem to be doing it for the potential reward.

It was this explanation the Western media found nearly impossible to understand. In other disasters, such as floods elsewhere and Hur-

They did it because it was the right thing to do.

ricane Katrina in New Orleans, there had been widespread looting. Desperate people anywhere in the world will behave like desperate people. So the BBC asked the question others around the world were wondering: "Why is there no looting in Japan after the earthquake?"[18] The explanations were varied. Some credited the Japanese legal system, which rewards honesty more than others. Others said police presence or social norms were the reason.

What made it even more amazing, though, was that it was not the only example of how the Japanese people would show their unselfish side.

The earthquake and tsunami had also led to a series of equipment failures, nuclear meltdowns, and the release of radioactive materials at the Fukushima Daiichi nuclear power complex. The good news (if you could call it that) was that thanks to strict building standards and fail-safe systems, the effects of the earthquake were not disastrous. The total amount of radioactivity leaked, for example, was approximately one-tenth of what happened with Chernobyl in what is now the Ukraine.

Still, it was enough to keep Japan and the world on edge for months as the Japanese struggled to contain the leak. The massive cleanup effort was dangerous work. Immediately, thousands of workers diligently tried to improve containment and avoid greater damage by using seawater to cool the reactors. During the cleanup, more than 80,000 people were evacuated from their homes.

For weeks, the television in Japan would show images of mostly young men wearing protective suits and working in one of the most radioactive areas on Earth. For retired engineers Yasuteru Yamada and Nobuhiro Shiotani, it was a wake-up call; they had to do something.

In early April of 2011, they formed a group they called the "Skilled Veterans Corps" and sent out thousands of e-mails and letters to their community of colleagues. In a blog post, Yamada asked for people over 60 who have "the physical strength and experience to bear the burden of this front-line work." According to him, "it would benefit society if the older generation took the job because we will get less damage from working there."[19]

Almost overnight 400 people volunteered their services to Tokyo Electric Power (Tepco) to help with the cleanup. Over the next six months, the Skilled Veterans Corps would not only grow to more than 600 former scientists and engineers, they would become a media sensation. Their stories of selflessness and sacrifice were told by the CNN, BBC, *New York Times*, *Los Angeles Times*, and hundreds of other media outlets around the world.

While bureaucracy prevented the group from fully engaging and taking on the role they wanted, the example stands among one of the most heroic in recent memory of an older group choosing to put themselves into a dangerous situation to protect a younger group of men, most of whom they had no personal connection to.

Volunteering for one of the most dangerous jobs on earth or selflessly choosing to return millions of yen are extreme examples. They prove what people can do in the right circumstances if given the opportunity. Starting Operation Beautiful or creating a new networking group are examples that may feel more approachable, but in our daily lives most of us may not have the chance to do anything so profound.

One thing we do likely spend quite a bit of time doing, though, is interacting with companies that supply our product and services. What role could unselfishness take there? Could businesses that manage to behave in more unselfish ways on a daily basis really connect more deeply with us as consumers?

To find out, let's look at a platform that encourages billions of interactions every day with one simple caveat: They are each limited to 140 characters in length.

The Customer Service Revolution Will Be Twitterized

It was no secret to Carol Borghesi that using social media for customer care was a hot topic. She was about to take the stage to talk about her experiences at Telus, one of the largest telecommunications companies in Canada. The telecommunications industry in almost every part of the world is a perfect test case for the impact social media might have on how companies provide customer support and service. In several social media surveys, it is routinely rated as one of the most popular industries that people like to talk about online, along with restaurants and consumer electronics.

What they talk about, though, can vary widely. It might include everything from seeking advice on a new mobile phone to complaining about a dropped call or service-related problem. All of this conversation has certainly been causing a lot of confusion and anxiety in the business world.

In 2010, a survey conducted by SmartBrief and market research firm Summus Limited asked over 6,000 business executives how confident they felt in their social media strategies. The results were telling. Only 14.2 percent of businesses rated their social media strategies as "very effective," and only 7.3 percent consider them to be "very revenue generating." So that cold November day in 2011, some of the world's largest brands had gathered in New York to try and crack the code on using social media for better customer care by attending a summit organized by an organization conveniently called Useful Social Media.

Borghesi was one of the first speakers of the day. "Social media," she started, "is kind of like peeing in a dark suit. We're getting a warm feeling but no one else knows what is happening." The audience couldn't help but laugh in agreement. It was the perfect opening for the event because it shared the unspoken truth that no one really had the magic solution.

What they *had* all figured out, however, was that social media was changing something very fundamental about how they provided service to their customers. Along with Borghesi and Telus, other brands, including Coca Cola, Best Buy, KLM, Zappos, Comcast, and Samsung, took the stage to share the lessons they had learned about how to achieve effective social customer care and the results they were seeing on Twitter.

As the day went on, a surprising theme began to arise. The brands that were building relationships by creating the most engagement on Twitter were not just the ones who answered customer questions or complaints. That was the most basic requirement and you almost *had* to do it.

The more interesting conclusion was that many of the brands were proactively answering questions that consumers *hadn't asked them directly*. It was as if brands were calling up a customer at their home and answering a question they had asked a friend at a barbeque but never thought to ask a brand. And while this would have been extremely creepy through the phone, it was welcomed online.

The short format of Twitter allowed brands to connect with people in an unselfish way by offering a useful point of view that could proactively help a customer to answer a question or learn something new and interesting. In an audience filled with hundreds of marketing and customer care people desperate to create deeper customer connections, this lesson alone was worth the price of admission.

For a platform that blogger Chris Pirillo once jokingly described as "a great place to tell the world what you're thinking before you've had a chance to think about it," Twitter was turning out to be a stunningly effective tool for business to better appreciate and converse with their customers in an unselfish way.

Why We Are Selfish

We have seen throughout this chapter that being unselfish is an important human trait and one that people naturally gravitate toward. Whether you are looking at the rise of more compassionate care in medicine or how an entire country responds to a natural disaster—the quality of being unselfish is a necessary step towards building more trust because it enables deeper more personal relationships.

There are more examples today of global unselfishness and collaboration than at any other time in human history. Yet in our daily interactions, many of us might still experience situations where people or companies still behave in selfish ways. Here are a few common reasons why this still happens:

1. **Assuming a zero-sum game.** The most common reason people behave in selfish ways is because of the common assumption that if you win, that means I lose. It is the force that powers politicians to disagree on the simplest of things, and why companies implement silly policies like making sure you can't return a product even if it didn't work when you bought it. This winner and loser mentality persists because, in some situations, it is actually true. Often, though, what may be true immediately is not true later. For example, if I charge you more for a bottle of water today, the fact is I will make more money. The real problem is that you may not come back to buy from me again.

2. **Wanting to get without giving.** The most common definition of selfishness involves people expecting something from others without reciprocating. Reciprocity is an important social behavioral principle that drives much of what we do, and when it is missing, this usually leads to one group feeling the other is selfish.

3. **"Short-Termism."** One of the biggest criticisms of capitalism for some time has been how it tends to force companies and people to look only at short-term results instead of long-term effects. Focusing on the short term will often inherently lead to selfishness because you are only concerned about what happens right away and not in the future.

For every example of unselfish behavior on the part of a brand or a person, the true test comes from the motivation behind it. It is not that difficult to behave unselfishly when you know you will be rewarded for doing so, or if you are expecting something in return. However, this is not authentic altruism; the key is to find a way to be authentically unselfish.

The Three Elements of Unselfishness

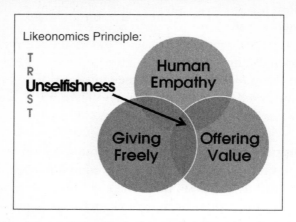

Likeonomics Principle:

T
R
U **Unselfishness**
S
T

It is not often that you hear someone ask to pay more taxes. Yet, billionaire investor Warren Buffett has said over and over again that he would prefer to pay more taxes, and he isn't alone. A survey in 2011 from Spectrem Group reported that 68 percent of millionaires (people with investments of $1 million or more) supported raising taxes on those with $1 million or more in income. This desire to give back also led Buffet to work with the Bill and Melinda Gates Foundation to create the Giving Pledge. Described as an effort to get the wealthiest people in the world to help solve the biggest problems in society, the pledge encourages billionaires to promise to give at least half of their wealth to charity during their lifetimes or upon their death. Over 40 families have signed up so far.

Human Empathy	Giving Freely	Offering Value
There is no substitute for actually caring, and that requires a level of empathy where you can relate to someone on a human level.	True unselfishness requires giving without expectations for something in return. Nothing can poison an unselfish act quicker than the sense you are only doing it in exchange for something else.	When you can offer value through answering a question or providing service in an unexpected way, you can make unselfishness tangible in a powerful and necessary way.

Buffet could not have launched the Giving Pledge if he didn't actually care about the world around him. Others would not have joined him if they didn't share that same attitude.

When an unselfish act starts, it comes from a basis of human empathy.

The action itself is not enough, though. Most of us know people who would gladly do something which appears to be like an unselfish act, but is actually only a down payment that they are expecting to get back in some way. Nothing can poison an unselfish act more than giving people the sense that you are expecting something from them in return. You need to be able to give freely.

The problem is, it is common for there to be expectations. Large political donations, for example, are almost always given by people who have some type of expectations from political candidates if they manage to win and get into office. This issue was the main motivation behind the creation of Maplight.org, a website that gathers public data in order to reveal the influence of money on politics and how politicians vote. Belief never comes from this type of quid pro quo.

The final element of unselfishness is offering some kind of tangible value. In Japan, the citizens volunteered to help cleanup the radiation. Doctors who man-

An act becomes unselfish only without the expectation of a "karmic kickback" or end goal of benefitting yourself.

age to be kind and compassionate even when their busy schedules offer them every reason not to be stand out. They are rewarded with loyalty from patients who refuse to sue them, and they don't engage in such selfless behavior because it is a good risk-management strategy.

They do it because it is the right thing to do, and despite what it may seem like on occasion, we still live in a world where that makes a difference in success or failure. Doing the right thing is good business and good living, too.

CHAPTER SUMMARY
THREE THINGS TO REMEMBER ABOUT UNSELFISHNESS

1. Ethical companies that run their business based on ideals consistently have a long-term edge and outperform companies who do not make this a priority. More and more consumers have begun to expect companies to behave in this way, and reward those companies with their loyalty.
2. People have an inherent ability to be altruistic and this can lead to many positive effects in the world, from sharing experiences to helping others to collecting the world's knowledge together into a vast encyclopedia of human knowledge.
3. Beyond compassion, being unselfish also means offering something of value (such as expertise) without expectation of some sort of "karmic kickback."

Online Workbook and Action Guide:
How to Be More Unselfish

www.likeonomics.com/unselfish

Simplicity

"Perfection is achieved not when there is nothing left to add but when there is nothing left to take away."

— Antoine de Saint-Exupéry, French aviator,
writer, and poet

"Simplicity is the ultimate sophistication."

— Leonardo da Vinci

In 2001, the world's best dinner party was about to change forever. What started as one of the most exclusive invite-only gatherings of big thinkers, celebrities, and influential people interested in sharing world-changing ideas had grown year after year to become one of the most respected events in the world. The rules of the event were simple; there was only ever one track of speakers, so that all the attendees would have a shared experience to speak about. The second rule was the one that would become the calling card for the entire event; every talk had to be no more than 18 minutes long.

By now you may have figured out that the event was the TED conference, originally started in 1984 by Richard Saul Wurman. In 2001 the event had grown into an interesting problem . . . its exclusive closed-door format was actually hindering its mission to encourage the sharing of world-changing ideas. Something had to change.

That same year Wurman was turning 65 years old and ready to pass on the torch to a new curator of the event. Media entrepreneur, *WIRED Magazine* editor, and TED enthusiast Chris Anderson was the perfect candidate. Anderson purchased the event and took over that year, instituting three important changes that would dramatically change the future of TED:

1. The addition of a sister conference, TEDGlobal, held in a different country every other year.
2. Creation of the TED Prize, which grants its winners one wish to change the world.
3. A groundbreaking audio and video podcast series, TEDTalks, in which the best TED content is released free online.

It was the last item on this list that worried the TED team the most. After all, if they just released the talks for free online, would people still see the value in paying thousands of dollars in order to attend in person? Despite the risk, they decided to proceed anyway. In 2006, executive producer of TED Media June Cohen led the effort to post videos of TED talks online. "Friends of mine thought it was professional suicide," Cohen recalls. "It was not at all obvious that there was an audience for taped lectures online."

When posting them, they projected that the videos would see less than 100,000 views (using a podcast from Malcolm Gladwell that had been downloaded 40,000 times as a baseline). They underestimated. That first year, the talks were downloaded 10.5 million times. Simultaneously, the fees to attend the conference were also raised by 50 percent and the event *still* sold out within a week, and had a 1,000-person waiting list to get in.

Today, the TED brand and TED talks in particular are some of the most popular videos consistently watched online. The idea of TED has also been licensed so anyone can create their own local "TEDx" event assuming they adhere to a small number of guidelines. In September of 2010, an article in *Fast Company* called TED "the new Harvard—only bigger."[1]

What had turned TED into such a global phenomenon? Was it all about having great speakers? Did it come down to agreeing to share free content online and licensing the model to other events without cost? In his opening remarks at TED in 2011, Chris Anderson spoke about the fact that nearly every idea about how to deal with the biggest problems in the world is invariably crushed by cynicism or complexity.

In her recap of the event that year, journalist Ariana Huffington recalled asking Anderson which of the sessions that day would most directly counter the big issue he had spoken about. "Session 11," he predicted. "It's the one on simplicity. We are choking ourselves in a web of complexity. Our financial system is so complex it can't be regulated. The health care plan is so complex no one understands it. Our politics is so complex it's become a complete mess." The session he mentioned was one given by the chemist George Whitesides, on the science of simplicity.

Perhaps without intending to, Anderson had also pointed out what may be the biggest factor in the popularity of TED and the "ideas worth sharing" that the event and brand is known for: Every talk has a built in simplicity, because the longest anyone can ever speak for is 18 minutes. It is a powerful reminder that there are only a few organizations or experiences in our world today that are so consistently devoted to maintaining this sort of simplicity.

Desperately Seeking Simplicity

There is a reason why Google has religiously resisted the temptation to put anything on their home page besides a text box and a search button. Simplicity for Google is a defining principle. It was also the quality that many appreciated most about the late Steve Jobs. Longtime partner and Apple co-founder Steve Wozniak was often quoted speaking about how he felt Jobs's real skill and genius was in making things truly simple.

Jobs himself once said, "Simple can be harder than complex: You have to work hard to get your thinking clean to make it simple. But it's worth it in the end because once you get there, you can move mountains."[2]

Apart from a few heroic stories and visionary leaders, though, simplicity is surprisingly hard to implement in practice. We tend to overcomplicate our lives, worrying about things we shouldn't and "sweating the small stuff" even though we have plenty of advice telling us not to do so. Companies make far too many products and overload their consumers. Already, in earlier chapters, we have seen plenty of examples of product overload and store shelves that are filled with too much complexity.

We have also learned throughout school that complexity may, in the right situations, even make us seem more intelligent—for example, by using more complex words in a term paper. To explore this point specifically, a Princeton University researcher named Daniel M. Oppenheimer conducted a fascinating experiment in 2005 which should be required reading for any college professor handing out writing assignments to students.

In the experiment, undergraduate students were asked to share how often they would use larger words in writing assignments in order to appear more intelligent. The vast majority admitted to doing this often. Fueled by their confessions, Oppenheimer then analyzed how people who *read* those same assignments were likely to describe the intelligence of the person writing them. You would expect, as most of us are taught, that using big words and using them correctly would add to your intelligence score. Instead, Oppenheimer uncovered an *inverse* relationship between complexity and judged intelligence.

In other words, the bigger words you used, the dumber people thought you were.

It was a finding that lawyer Alan Seigel echoed when he took the stage to deliver his own TED talk on the necessity of simplifying legal jargon. And he started his talk with a question that proves this point exactly:

> How is it we can run the country on a 16-page constitution, yet it takes 2,074 pages and more than 400,000 words of gobbledygook to present the Senate Health Care Bill?[3]

The solution he called for was to use more "plain English" in legal documents so we could reduce the complexity and "bring more humanity back into communications." Thankfully, this is a fight that has plenty of allies around the world.

The Plain Language Movement

Annetta Cheek is a 25-year veteran of the federal government who now runs a nonprofit called the Center for Plain Language. There has never been a more important time for the Center to exist. "When you're supposed to be a democracy, and people don't even understand what government is doing, that's a problem,"[4] Cheek says. This is not just an American problem either.

All across the world, people are wasting countless hours dealing with bureaucracy and complexity on every level. In 2010, the Hong Kong–based group Political and Economic Risk Consultancy surveyed more than 1,300 business executives in 12 Asian countries. In the results, India was named for having a bureaucratic system that was "one of the most stifling in the world."[5] The report cited a strong correlation between an inefficient bureaucracy and high corruption rates.

Sweden, in contrast, enjoys very low corruption and has been credited as being one of the first cultures to recognize the power of natural language. Way back in 1713, King Charles XII of Sweden dictated this ordinance:

> *His Majesty the King requires that the Royal Chancellery in all written documents endeavour to write in clear, plain Swedish and not to use, as far as possible, foreign words.*[6]

Today, more than half of all Swedish government authorities are involved in plain language projects. The Swedish government has a linguist in the Cabinet Office, and a division whose responsibility is to review government documents and ensure natural language is used before allowing them to be distributed widely. In other governments across the world, there is a lot of support for the plain language movement, as well.

Recently in the United States, the government passed the Plain Writing Act of 2010, which requires all federal government agencies to use plain language in every covered document and train federal workers on how to use plain language. A year later, when the Center for Plain Language announced the winners of their annual ClearMark award for plain language, the IRS was the unlikely choice as Grand Prize winner.

The Myth of Good Complexity

When it comes to most government organizations, hardly anyone *wants* more complexity in documents. Typically when you end up with bills featuring thousands of pages of content, it is because large armies of people worked on writing them, or because no one took the time to make them succinct and clear.

In business, however, there can be the real possibility that some complexity exists because it is seen to be valuable in some misguided way. Brands launch

> **In other words, the reason for complexity in government typically comes down to either inefficiency or laziness.**

more product extensions because they think consumers want more choice. Lawyers add 30-page disclaimers and terms and conditions in an effort to shield the company from some unforeseen liability or potential lawsuits. Airlines are notorious for having dozens of different flight "*fare codes*" so they can offer varying rates to different types of travelers based on when they book and other factors.

Unfortunately I have sat in plenty of meetings with very smart business people who argue passionately to keep the complexity in their business because they believe they need to have it. Here are a few of the arguments they usually use:

1. Our business is inherently complex.
2. Our customers are smart and they get it.
3. We need the complexity in order to make money.
4. It would be impossible to get the right people to agree to simplify.

No matter how forceful the arguments, "good complexity" in most forms usually turns out to be a myth. There are probably certain situations today where complexity may not be causing any serious problems . . . yet. As the consumer electronics industry has been learning for the past decade, the problem is that just because complexity isn't killing you right now, that doesn't mean it never will.

Gadget Confusion

A few months ago, I searched on Amazon to find a new Blu-Ray player and found 335 different models. When I went that same day to check the price of a mobile phone I had seen several months ago, I found that it was no longer offered and there was a brand new, barely distinguishable model available in its place.

TVs have become so complicated now that many manufacturers of high-end sets recommend you pay several hundred dollars (on top of buying the TV) for a "calibration service" just to make

> **If you purchased a digital camera just six months ago, chances are if you walked into an electronics retailer they would no longer offer it for sale.**

sure all of the settings are optimized for your TV once you get it home. This constant complexity leads to gadget confusion, where competing products differ only slightly and consumers end up bewildered and frustrated.

In response to the growing epidemic of gadget confusion, some retailers have created full "Geek Squads" of internal technical experts who can make house calls and help to set up or explain technology. In addition, a startup called Decide.com launched in 2011, and has already partnered with *Consumer Reports* to offer a tool that helps shoppers decide whether they should buy a gadget now or wait until the next upgraded replacement comes out.

One of the most interesting types of products to examine in this evolution of complexity is one that has managed to escape the trend of increasing complexity, and instead, offer products that are getting simpler and simpler: the handheld video camera.

When Sony launched the first consumer video camera in the early 1980s, it was so bulky that it was designed to rest on your shoulder in order to be "portable." The technology quickly evolved, though, and over the next 20 years, Sony and their competitors focused on two big priorities:

1. Make the video camera smaller.
2. Keep the recording quality as good as possible.

The products were still generally difficult to use, requiring you to wade through a user manual to learn how to use all the right buttons and features, but it was seen as a necessary evil.

The bigger problem was that consumers were all building up a vast but nearly useless library of video on tapes or data cards. After forcing some immediate family or unfortunate friends to watch those videos right away, they would be stuck on a shelf or in a drawer waiting for the day when you would finally return to edit them. The day usually never came.

Then, in 2007, a single product changed everything.

Flipping the Video Camera Market

A small startup named Pure Digital had first launched a product in 2006 called the "Pure Digital Point & Shoot" video camcorder, which was exclusively available at CVS pharmacies. It was a one-time-use video camera designed to enable you to record video and then bring it back to your local CVS to have it turned into a DVD.

A year later, the camera was relaunched as a permanent camera that most industry analysts thought wouldn't last a month. The video quality wasn't great. The price point was less than one-third of other video cameras on the market. Even the design of this little product looked like a toy, with just one simple red button at the back and barely any instructions. It was that easy to use.

As founder Jonathan Kaplan would later explain, "The really successful [products] are ones people never thought they wanted."[7] And Kaplan's product did have one killer feature aside from its simplicity of use: a built-in USB plug that would allow users to easily plug the camera directly into their computers in order to upload or edit videos easily using the built-in software.

> **The most important thing about video wasn't the picture quality. It was how simple it was to take and how easily you could share it with the people in your life.**

Realizing that the product's name would be a vital component, Pure Digital hired a naming company, which developed hundreds of potential names. The name Kaplan gave to the product, though, was inspired by the keychain to his Audi and how the spring-loaded key would pop out at the touch of a button. He named the new camera *Flip*.

On September 12, 2007, the Flip Ultra camera was released. It instantly vaulted to become the best-selling camcorder on Amazon.com, and it stayed there. In less than two years, they sold more than 1 million cameras and became a household name. Their success led the company to be acquired for $590 million in 2008, an amazing feat for a small startup that had only launched its flagship product two years earlier.

Ultimately, in 2011, a number of forces contributed to the Flip video product line being discontinued, including rapid growth in video technology built into mobile

> **Simplicity could trump everything else. Simplicity, in other words, could be the ultimate competitive advantage.**

phones, as well as more point and shoot digital cameras including high-quality video. By then, Sony, Canon, and many other competitors also had launched their own cameras with a similar flip-out style USB connection. Yet despite being shuttered, the impact of the Flip camera (and the value of simplicity) on the technology world was clear.

Winning on Simplicity

The power of simplicity was something that Gerard Kleisterlee recognized earlier than most. In May of 2001, he took over as CEO of Royal Philips Electronics. That year, the dot-com bubble burst and shrunken consumer spending following the World Trade Center attack in September contributed to Philips losing $3.9 billion. The following year they lost another $3 billion, despite cutting about 55,000 employees.

Needing desperately to turn the company around, Kleisterlee set a bold new vision that would refocus the company on two key qualities: innovation and simplicity. Innovation, in many ways, would be the easy part. With over 100,000 patents filed since the company's founding in 1891 by two brothers in the Netherlands, Philips was widely considered one of the world's most innovative companies.

Simplicity would be harder. For Kleisterlee, simplicity in technology had a clear definition, and it had everything to do with ease of use.

Internally, the following description was circulated for evaluating every product:

> *Ease of operation: product interfaces should be logical, simple to understand, simple to operate, and intuitive. Consumers should spend the least amount of time referring to a manual of instruction.*[8]

Changing the reality was only the first piece of Philips transformation, though. Chief Marketing Officer Andrea Ragnetti was then challenged to transform how Philips would communicate their simplicity message throughout everything they did from a communications point of view. The first thing Ragnetti did to make this real was to assemble a "Simplicity Advisory Board" in 2004. It was made up of an eclectic mix of experts, from a young fashion designer named Sara Berman to a Japanese visual arts professor named Ken Okuyama.

Together with this advisory board, Ragnetti launched a multi-year campaign, which would feature testimonials, conversations with creative personalities, online video, and global advertising. Their philosophy extended far beyond simplifying their own products. They purchased all the advertising for an entire episode of *60 Minutes* for $2 million, and instead of running ads, they "donated" the extra time back to viewers so people could enjoy more of the news program without interruption. Their aim wasn't just to simplify their products, but to do what they could to *simplify our lives.*

The campaign and philosophy offered a bigger vision of the world and what mattered to the brand. It was their "big ideaL," as my Ogilvy colleagues would call it. And it worked. According to Interbrand rankings of the best global brands, Philips moved from being ranked No. 65 in 2004 to No. 41 in 2011, doubling their brand value from $4.378 billion in 2004 to $8.658 billion in 2011.

As CEO Kleisterlee explained, "Philips is not the only technology company to grasp the need for simplicity—but I believe we're the first to put a stake in the ground and declare our intent to take action. Others may aspire to be more fashionable, more cool. Our route to innovation isn't about extra complexity—it's about simplicity, which we believe will be the new cool."[9]

How Simplicity Inspires Trust

No one was likely more pleased about seeing a real tangible case study of a business succeeding because of its focus on simplicity than former MIT professor and current president of the Rhode Island School of Design John Maeda. He was also one of the five original members of Philips' Simplicity Advisory Board and the one who had most directly devoted his expertise and career to studying the impact of simplicity in our everyday lives. As a well-known advocate of why technology needs more simplicity, he was named one of the 75 most influential people of the twenty-first century by *Esquire* magazine and called the "Steve Jobs of academia" by *Forbes* magazine.[10]

In 2006, he published a book called *The Laws of Simplicity*, in which he proposed 10 laws for balancing simplicity and complexity in business, technology, and design. The book quickly became required reading among product designers around the world and has since been translated into 14 languages.

Two of his laws in particular stood out for me as powerful concepts, which also apply to the overall idea of Likeonomics and why simplicity is such an important principle:

- **Law #1—Reduce:** The simplest way to achieve simplicity is through thoughtful reduction.
- **Law #8—Trust:** In simplicity we trust.

Reduction, on a basic level, was one of the core design principles that helped many of Apple's products to do well and stand out. The third generation iPod shuffle, for example, featured a buttonless design and was perhaps the most relentlessly reduced product ever manufactured. Despite having a few buttons, the Flip Cam was another product that succeeded because of its focus on simplification and reduction.

More than any other, Maeda's eighth law is the idea that echoes the main premise of this chapter.

One powerful example of putting those pieces together comes from the Canadian bank ING Direct,

> Simplicity can help lead to more trust and less confusion.

which has grown over the past decade to become the number one largest online bank in America.

How Orange Got People Saving Again

The one number that makes ING Direct CEO Arkadi Kuhlmann happiest is $11.2 billion. For a banker to be happy about a large amount of money isn't too surprising, until you learn that the number Kuhlmann is so thrilled about isn't what his bank has earned, but rather what they have paid out to their customers in interest since first offering their no-frills savings accounts back in 2000.

At a comparable bank with similar money under management, the interest payments over that period would usually account for only $2 billion, making ING Direct one of the most generous options in the banking industry for helping people to save money.[11] They are not just taking less money, though.

The model for ING Direct is dramatically simplified. They have no physical locations, reduced services, and let their customers access all their money online. As a result, their costs can be far lower than those of a traditional bank.

In 2000, when Kuhlmann was considering expanding the bank from its highly successful debut in his native Canada, the U.S. market was the natural extension. It would be difficult, though, as the United States was a much more crowded market. In order to stand out, he knew they needed to have a simple message. As he notes in his book *The Orange Code*:

> If we were leading Americans back to savings, then how would we help accomplish this? That debate was even tougher. Good service, good prices? Everyone claims this so we would just not be believable. So, instead, we would simplify. We would make our product simple, allowing customers to save time and money.[12]

With this philosophy, they launched the company with the mission to "lead Americans back to saving" at its heart. Just over a decade later, the results speak for themselves. Under Kuhlmann's leadership, ING

Direct grew into the country's largest savings bank with more than $88 billion in assets, and more than 7.7 million customers.

While the U.S. business was sold to Capital One in 2011, the core philosophy has remained the same. If you visit the ING Direct headquarters, for example, a sign outside reads, "Simplify, Simplify, Simplify." This is a core belief at ING Direct, where the mission has always been clear: "Save them money or save them time."

Hypnotizing Chickens

Anyone who says that a picture is worth a thousand words hasn't spent much time looking at military documents or speaking with General Stanley A. McChrystal of the U.S. Armed Forces. In 2009, as the leader of American and NATO forces in Afghanistan, he was shown a slide of an image that was meant to show the complexity of the American military strategy for Afghanistan Stability." The image looked more like a bowl of spaghetti, prompting General McChrystal to note, "When we understand that slide, we'll have won the war."[13]

PowerPoint is a commonly used tool in military and political meetings to reduce complex ideas into bite-sized pieces that can be consumed quickly in order to make decisions. Everyone from political leaders to military commanders use them as shorthand to try and understand issues when there isn't enough time to read full briefing reports. The problem is, sometimes in the process of simplifying, the message itself gets lost.

In the summer of 2009, retired Marine colonel Thomas X. Hammes published an article in the *Armed Forces Journal* titled "Dumb-Dumb Bullets," in which he cautioned against the overuse of PowerPoint in the military. PowerPoint, he wrote, "is not a neutral tool—it is actively hostile to thoughtful decision making."[14] General James N. Mattis went even further while on stage at a military conference in North Carolina, saying, "PowerPoint makes us stupid."

Criticizing PowerPoint is a popular pastime in business, as well, where people use terms like *PowerPoint hell* or *death by PowerPoint* to describe how the common use of too many bullet points can obscure the real point the presenter is trying to make.

As a final ironic joke, there *is* one situation where the military has found great value in PowerPoint presentations: briefing reporters. They often use the slang term *hypnotizing chickens* to describe the common situation of using 20 minutes of extremely boring and nonsensical PowerPoint slides in order to "bore their audience into a coma" when they don't want to reveal any *real* information.

But aside from this one intentionally complex use by the military, does PowerPoint really deserve all the abuse we give it? After all, if someone creates a boring film, we don't tend to blame the camera, do we?

How Napkins Can Explain Health Care

If you ask Dan Roam, it's not a PowerPoint problem that's killing us; it's a word problem. His philosophy is perfectly summarized in the title of his third book: *Blah, Blah Blah: What to Do When Words Won't Work*. Roam is the best-selling author of *Back of the Napkin* and an expert on visual thinking and how to solve complicated problems with pictures.

As a consultant to some of the world's largest companies, his gift is the ability to take complicated issues and simplify them in a *meaningful* way.

> **Making something simpler is *not* the same thing as making it shorter or even just making it easier.**

As we saw with the military examples, simplifying without maintaining a relevant message can lead to useless bullet points and indecipherable pasta-shaped charts.

To illustrate the power of using meaningful images, Roam participated in a contest in 2009, put on by Slideshare.com (a website that describes itself as the "YouTube of PowerPoint"). The site makes it easy for anyone to upload their presentations to share with the world and embed into any other website. It has also become one of the leading online resources and advocates for a world filled with better and less boring presentations.

In addition to resources to help anyone improve their presentations, the competetion Slideshare hosts is an annual search to find great

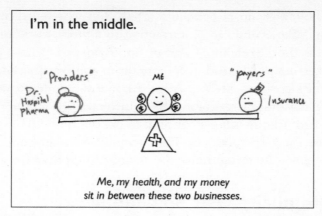

Figure 7.1 Mission Possible: Dan Roam Simplifies the US Healthcare System

Courtesy of Dan Roam.

presentations called "The World's Best Presentation Contest." Roam's entry to the contest was a collaboration with physician and health-care strategist C. Anthony Jones, which was designed to explain how health care worked in America. Through a series of images, he explained how the health-care system was dependent on three critical groups—the "*providers*" (docs, hospitals and pharma), the "*payers*" (insurance companies), and the *patients* (you). The challenge in health care, he noted, is that you are stuck between the providers and the payers, and they both want your money (Figure 7.1).

It was a brilliantly simple way to explain a topic that was (and still is!) confusing millions of Americans as they were hearing about health care reform but not really understanding the options or the proposals that politicians were making. His presentation won the competition easily, and has been seen hundreds of thousands of times.

There are plenty of signs that the popularity of visual thinking extends far beyond a few pioneering management consultants, as well:

• In the Netherlands, Dutch psychologists have founded a nonprofit organization called the "Maria J. Krabbe Stichting Beelddenken" to study the phenomena of *picture thinking* and whether there may be some portion of our population who predominantly think in terms of pictures.

- Since 2009, a group of designers, artists, and writers led by graphic designer Mike Rohde are contributing to a worldwide community known as the "Sketchnote Army" for *sketchnoters* (those who use visual sketches to take and share notes from conferences and events).
- Ad agency creative director Andy Azula created demo tapes of a series of new commercials for UPS, which featured him in front of a whiteboard drawing simple concepts to explain how UPS could help their customers' bottom lines. The client loved the ads, and ended up casting him as the recognizable sketch artist featured in the ads, too.

Why Simplicity Gets So Complicated

If you spend too much time looking at sketch notes or great distillations of complex ideas into easy visuals, you can't help thinking the simplicity should be easy. In reality, simple is far from easy. Getting to a simple concept in whatever form you have it is often a difficult and time-consuming task. As I usually tell my students, writing a great short piece is much more difficult than writing a decent long one.

It is the reason I never require them to write a minimum number of words for any writing assignment or blog post. If they can make a comprehensive and convincing argument in a sentence or a tweet, what is the point in asking them to write more? So far, no one has managed to deliver a great point of view just in a single sentence—but the policy has encouraged them all to think about saying more with less words.

Here are a few of the reasons why focusing on making things simple can actually be really hard:

1. **Beware the curse of knowledge.** When you know a topic well, it is easy for you to think that you are simplifying something when actually you are not. In *Made to Stick*, Chip and Dan Heath referred to this as the curse of knowledge. They note, "We start to forget what it is like *not* to know what we know. Simplifying, we fear, can devolve into oversimplifying."[15]
2. **Simplifying requires focus, not a specific skill.** When you are effectively simplifying an idea or message, it might seem like only a select group of consultants or experienced message creators can really do it. This is far from the truth. Simplicity in any sense is an end goal that any team or individual can reach, as long as you have the right focus.

3. **Saying less can take more time.** Good simplification is rarely a quick process. The reason is because often it requires you to spend time figuring out all the things that you won't do, or all the features that you won't build. Remember that real simplicity can be a process of elimination, where you are only left with the most important ideas or features at the end.

We tend to hear over and over from focused leaders that simplicity is more driven by what you decide to leave out rather than what you keep. John Maeda focused on reduction as his first law of simplicity. In that process, it can be easy to lose meaning or reduce the wrong things. For that reason, what really matters is not just making something simple, but also ensuring that the best ideas and elements of an idea or business are not lost.

The Three Elements of Simplicity

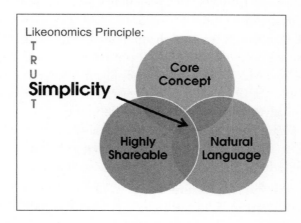

When Sakichi Toyoda founded Toyota Industries in 1926, he brought with him an idea that has since become legendary in the world of manufacturing and beyond. Known widely as the concept of the *"five whys,"* his idea was that if any problem occurs, simply asking *why* five times to each answer you come up with will usually be enough to get to the root cause of the problem.

It is a simple and often repeated technique used to simplify problems so they could be more easily solved in a complex manufacturing environment. The same idea works when it comes to simplifying to help you get to the core idea or message. The aim is an idea that is, as Einstein once said, "as simple as possible, and no simpler."

Core Concept	Highly Shareable	Natural Language
When you have distilled the complexity around you into a single clear concept that you can easily explain, you have found the core that matters.	Making anything shareable will be the way that the simplicity you have defined will be able to spread.	Speaking in a plain way without using overly academic words is a critical element in making anything simple enough for people to truly understand.

When Frank Batten and John Coleman had the crazy idea in 1982 to start an entire cable television channel dedicated to nothing but weather 24 hours a day, cable network executives said they were crazy. What kind of audience would watch a channel just about weather? The channel had a strong core concept and idea of what it would do, however, and launched on May 2, 1982, with the slogan "We Take the Weather Seriously, but not Ourselves." This year, the network is celebrating its thirtieth anniversary of continual programming.

Simple ideas also tend to be highly shareable from person to person and so this is the critical second element of achieving simplicity—building something so simple that the most important people you should care about, from your customers to your employees, can easily understand and adopt the ideas into their lives as well as tell others about them.

The final piece is one that we spent quite a bit of time talking about in this chapter and that is used throughout this book: The power of natural language can be huge when it comes to building a more human connection with people.

One example of this is proverbs that are often repeated from person to person and convey a simple meaning in a way that uses natural language. "The early bird catches the worm" is one common example in which the proverb conveys meaning, but does it in a nonthreatening way.

Natural language means not only speaking like a real person in every real life interaction as well as any written communications you have online or offline, but also paying attention to how that language sounds when it is read aloud. One of my favorite tricks to make sure language stays natural is to take any written content and read it out loud. In doing this, you'll spot right away where it is natural and where it isn't.

CHAPTER SUMMARY
THREE THINGS TO REMEMBER ABOUT SIMPLICITY

1. Complexity can sometimes be described as a good or necessary thing. Usually, it isn't. When you can simplify an idea or a product or a service, it becomes easier to remember, better to do, and more clear overall.
2. Often, the best simplicity can come from reduction, where you are able to take away any layers or activities that don't matter and focus only on the main core.
3. In professional and personal contexts, the power of visual thinking and drawing pictures instead of just using words can be the perfect way to simplify ideas and make them understood by a wider variety of people.

Online Workbook and Action Guide:
How to Be More Simple

www.likeonomics.com/simplicity

Timing

I am aware that success is more than a good idea. It is timing, too.
— Anita Roddick, founder of The Body Shop

Your best work involves timing. If someone wrote the best hip hop song of all time in the Middle Ages, he had bad timing.
— Scott Adams, creator of *Dilbert*

In 1855, a Scottish clergyman named James Gall had an idea that should have changed every map ever created, but didn't. It was four years before Charles Darwin would publish his *Origin of Species*, and Gall was presenting his world-changing idea at a Glasgow meeting of the British Association for the Advancement of Science. The world he lived in had long since evolved from the point where people thought Earth was flat.

The most commonly used map of the time was known as the Mercator map and was originally developed to help sailors to navigate the ocean and reach their destinations. It had been used for hundreds of years. There was only one problem . . . it was wrong.

In taking a spherical globe and projecting it onto a flat piece of paper, the sizes of the landmasses were distorted. Greenland, for example, looked huge while Africa appeared much smaller. In reality, Africa's landmass was nearly 13 times the size of Greenland. Gall's theory corrected this "projection problem" and adjusted the size of the landmasses—but it was too radical for his time. He and his map were widely ignored, and would be forgotten over the next thirty years.

Then, in 1885, the first inaugural issue of *The Scottish Geographical Magazine* was set to be published. Resolved to give it one more try,

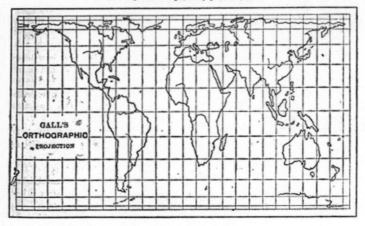

Figure 8.1   Gall's Orthographic Projection

Source: The Scottish Geographical Magazine (April 1885): 120.

Gall named his theory the "Gall Orthographic Projection" and wrote an article about it for the magazine (see Figure 8.1). When published, it unfortunately met with the same fate as before and was quickly dismissed. What did a reverend from Scotland know of cartography anyway? Time and history would forget Gall and his map projection again—this time for nearly 100 years, until something interesting happened in 1974.

That year, a German historian named Arno Peters proposed an almost identical idea that he had developed independently without knowing of Gall's work. His projected map appeared to be nearly the same as Gall's, and was based on similar calculations of longitude and latitude. But Peters' map (which *he* called the "Peters projection map") was introduced at a much different time in history.

In 1974, the world was consumed by the promise of racial and political equality. People had lived through two world wars, numerous revolutions, and race and gender rights were hot topics. The Peters projection map was seen to offer a symbol of hope and redemption for cultures around the world that had been colonized by Western nations. For many, it offered proof of the skewed worldview that many Western countries still held toward the rest of the developing world. It even found some advocates in the Western world itself.

Over the next decade and a half, controversy and intense debate followed the map everywhere. The former Chancellor of West Germany Willy Brandt used the map as a symbol of the equality of nations. The map was circulated among regional offices of the United Nations and other global organizations to be displayed on the wall. Gall's original map idea, meanwhile, had resurfaced thanks to his published article, and cartographers started referring to the new combined map as the "Gall–Peters Projection map"—the name it is known by today.

Despite the controversy, political pressure, and plain inertia keeping it from widespread adoption, the map has never really died. Over the three decades since it was introduced, the map has been featured in the American serial drama *The West Wing* and often used by military strategist Thomas Barnett on C-SPAN. In 1990 it even led a group of the most respected geographic organizations in the world to issue a recommendation to "strongly urge book and map publishers, the media and government agencies to cease using rectangular world maps for general purposes or artistic displays."

Today, while the Peters projection map is not considered the standard, it has been credited by academic and creator of *The History of Cartography Project* J. Brian Hartley with sparking the global debate around the political implications of maps and cartography. Gall, meanwhile, is only remembered ceremoniously in the merged name of the map.

Why did two men with almost identical ideas have such differing levels of success when introducing their respective ideas to the world? The reason Peters was able to succeed at getting worldwide recognition and inspire an international debate while Gall was largely forgotten is all about the importance of timing, and it explains a lot more than just the history of cartography.

The Most Creative Lunch in History

In the fall of 1994, Microsoft was moments away from buying Pixar. Yes, you read that right. It was a year before the first *Toy Story* movie was released, and Pixar was bleeding money. *Toy Story* was running $6 million over budget and Steve Jobs had already put nearly $50 million of his own money into Pixar. It seemed like a lost cause. Desperate to salvage any part of his investment, Jobs had told his team to speak with any interested buyers.

Nathan Myhrvold was interested. As Microsoft's technology evangelist, his job was to seek out new and promising technology. Pixar had something that easily fit the bill. In order to create the complex graphics required for their upcoming film, they had built an extremely advanced 3D graphic design software called *PhotoRealistic RenderMan*, or *PRMan* for short.

PRMan was the perfect software to help Windows programs power higher end graphics, and Myhrvold was ready to sign a deal. As the Pixar team prepared for the meeting, they pulled together one of the first completed scenes from the yet-to-be-completed *Toy Story* film to share with Myhrvold as well. The scene was the march of the green army men and their rope drop from the second floor. The plan was to use this sneak peek as a chance to try and get Myhrvold interested in buying the studio arm of Pixar as well as the PRMan software. Unfortunately, he didn't bite.

Filmmaking wasn't really Microsoft's core business. He just wanted PRMan. It was Jobs, however, who would pull back from the negotiations abruptly and decide not to sell anything. As Pixar employee Pam Kerwin would later recall, "Steve kind of jerked back because, I think, there was something visceral in him that said, 'This is going to be really stupendous.'"[1]

It turned out his instincts were right and Pixar would go on to become the most successful animated film company in history. What Jobs didn't know was just a few months earlier, to plan for the future, the Pixar animation team had what may have been the most creative lunch in history.

Their animators were putting the finishing touches on *Toy Story*, and a small group including director John Lassiter and other creative team members were gathering to talk about what should come next. During that lunch, they came up with a list of new movie concepts that would eventually inspire three more blockbuster Pixar films: *A Bug's Life*, *Monsters Inc.*, and *WALL-E*. Together, these films would gross $2.2 billion at the box office and be nominated for 15 Academy Awards.

The story of the near death and meteoric rise of Pixar is a favorite of mine for several reasons. It includes everything from the triumph of creativity to the birth of an entire industry of computer-generated animation that would lead to some of the most entertaining films of the past two decades.

More than anything else, though, it is a story of the power of having the right timing. The inspiration for 10 years of filmmaking happened over a lunch meeting. The fleeting moment when a critical piece of Pixar was almost sold to Microsoft was also all about the pivotal timing of deciding to stay the course or sell the company.

Timing Is Everything

Everything from finding the love of your life to launching the next world-changing startup comes down to having the right timing. When powerful ideas or amazing products fail, it is often as a result of having the wrong timing. Timing is so important, in fact, that there are a growing number of business and academic experts who are dedicating their career to studying its importance.

Professor Stuart Albert is one of the leading academic minds focused on studying timing, and is currently writing a book on the topic. From the timing of music to why timing matters for business, he is one of a handful of academic experts looking at how and why timing matters so much. During a visit to the Waito Management School in New Zealand, Professor Albert shared an interesting observation from his research, "If Saddam Hussein had understood the importance of timing strategy, he would have won the first Persian Gulf war." Timing is that important.

By looking at thousands of examples of timing mistakes, he is building a compelling case for the importance of timing. The big question his book will likely focus on is how people can do a timing analysis in real time, and figure out the best timing to do something more quickly. Some places have figured out the patterns early. The entertainment industry, for example, has a method commonly known as pairing to try and manufacture the right timing to launch a new show.

Pairing describes the practice of placing a new television show directly before or after a hit television show so that a network can capitalize on an existing audience to launch the new show. When *Friends* first debuted in 1994, it was placed in the coveted 8 p.m. Thursday timeslot, right before *Seinfeld*. The move is widely seen as the main reason why the show was able to take off so quickly and become one of the most popular sitcoms in television history for 10 successful seasons.

It turns out that the entertainment industry actually offers a perfect environment from which to study the importance of timing not only because creating successful entertainment is largely based on the right timing, but also because timing is such an important element of comedy that TV shows have been faking it for decades, thanks largely to a man most of Hollywood has never heard of named Charley Douglass.

How Sweetening Changed Television History

In an industry known for its secrecy while a project is in development, Charley Douglass was paranoid even by Hollywood standards. The fact that very few people knew anything about the mysterious former CBS sound studio engineer was surprising, considering he worked with almost every television producer creating shows between the late 1950s and early 1970s.

During his early days as a sound engineer, Douglass was called upon to insert bits of laughter into programs at spots that seemed appropriate. Over time, he began to create his own library of audience laughter and finally created his *laff box* designed to add a soundtrack of laughter to programs. On his device, he could choose laughs by length, style, gender, and age, and used over 300 laughs recorded on 32 tape loops. When working with producers, he would get the ideas on where laughs were to be inserted, and then work secretly on "sweetening" the program by adding in laughs.

His work was controversial, as no producer or actor wanted to admit their audience wouldn't automatically know where to laugh without the benefit of the sweetening, but the numbers didn't lie. Shows that included the inserted laughs were hits, and those that chose to skip it failed quickly. By 1976, when television started using stereo sound, there were many other players creating laugh tracks and the practice was there to stay. Why were the manufactured laughs so important?

They were timing cues, and helped people watching a TV program at home to know when they should laugh. If you took a program that had a laugh track and watched it today without the added laughs, it would sound completely odd and not funny. The laugh tracks have become such an expected part of the timing for the programs that we are quite literally unable to enjoy certain shows without it.

But how important is this heritage of manufactured timing in a new world where we have more control over *when* we do certain activities than ever before?

Our Time-Shifted Culture

When I was in grade school, there were basically two kinds of standardized tests: the ones where you answered every question in order, and the ones where you could skip a hard question and come back to it later. That was about the closest you could get in school to controlling how you spent your own time.

The adult world for much of the past century wasn't that different. You had your working time, which generally meant nine to five for most people, and then your weekends off. There were exceptions, of course, but most people followed the pattern.

Today, we live in a time-shifted culture where you can move everything from when you eat to teleworking from anywhere to choosing when you watch, read, or skim your media. Consider the following:

- Apps like ReadItLater and Instapaper let you find and save articles for reading when you are ready to pay attention and read them.
- DVRs let us pause, rewind, and save live television to watch at our own convenience.
- A service called Timetosignoff offers a curated service to prepare a nightly e-mail with all the news from the day and reminders of things that you missed.
- Customer service happens on all channels (including social media as well as phone) and is expected to be available 24/7.
- Entire jobs are being done at various times of the day and teleworking has been rising in popularity for the past several years.

With all of this control that we now have over the time we spend doing almost anything, the importance of timing is even more critical with regard to what we choose to believe and what we don't. Especially when it comes to the retail industry.

Gilt and Luxury with an Expiration

All you have to do is say the word *time-share* to inspire feelings of anger and revulsion amongst hundreds of thousands of travelers who have suffered through high-pressure sales presentations about buying shares in a property in an exotic location. Is it any surprise that most of us hate the experience of being stuck in an awkward high-pressure sales situation for something that we often have no desire to buy?

The Little Red Book of Selling is one of the most popular books on sales ever. Author Jeffrey Gitomer has a mantra that he repeats often: "People don't like to be sold, but they love to buy." So what if that high-pressure, time-driven sales approach that backfires so often for time-shares and gym memberships could be transformed into a positive experience instead?

If anyone has cracked that code, it may be the team at Gilt.com, one of the most popular ecommerce sites launched over the past five years. Gilt is a luxury retailer that sells high-end products at discounted (but not ridiculous must-be-fake) rates. The pressure in the experience comes from an interesting twist. Once you add any item to your shopping cart, you only have 10 minutes to complete your purchase. Deals are announced daily through e-mails that are sent to members at noon, exactly, and many products sell out within minutes. Fifty percent of Gilt's deal revenue is generated in the first hour after a sale starts.

On mobile devices, the performance is even better. Many consumers launch the mobile app just seconds after getting a notification from Gilt of a new sale. From 2009 to 2010, Gilt's revenue rose from $170 million to $425 million, according to *Internet Retailer* magazine.

Why does Gilt's high-pressure sales tactic work where it would backfire in so many other industries? What they have uncovered is that there is an emotional thrill that comes along with finding the right product immediately. They are one of the few retailers that have managed to capture the thrill of an impulse buy with higher priced luxury items. More importantly, the site is a living example of how powerful a motivator timing can be in the right context.

The Rise of Shopper Marketing

When it comes to the retail market, brands have been studying the role of timing in how people make buying decisions for a long time. Procter & Gamble (P&G) has been one of the most aggressive, using extensive research on consumer behavior to drive everything from product packaging to its placement on retail shelves. In 2005, P&G isolated a consumer shopping moment, which they called the "first moment of truth." It referred to the three- to seven-second window of time when a consumer notices a product on a store shelf.

According to their research, this was the most crucial moment of the entire buying process. More interestingly, it was not a moment that P&G's huge spends on television advertising were directly impacting. Instead, it was all about the in-store retail experience. Encouraged, P&G went to their partners and shared this insight to ask them to think about how to better market to the "first moment of truth," or FMOT, as they abbreviated it for short.

P&G hired a director of FMOT and created a 15-person department at their headquarters in Cincinnati, Ohio, to manage the initiative across all their brands. Several advertising agencies have also created entire divisions for in-store marketing and devoted experts to thinking about FMOT. Each year, the percentage of advertising spending from big brands that goes toward in-store promotions or *shopper marketing*, as it is often called, goes higher and higher.

Research conducted by Arbitron Inc., a media research firm, notes that shoppers are more likely to recall an ad seen in a mall than one seen at home.[2] While people are influenced in the actual store, the timing of retail promotions also plays a heavy part in the success of retailers. After the 2011 November/December holiday season, according to an article in the *San Francisco Chronicle*, Gap, Target, and Kohl's reported disappointing same-store sales after mistiming promotions or running out of inventory during the holiday shopping season.[3]

When it comes to how we buy products and services, the fact is that timing may be the most important quality of all. What makes this point even more significant is that this all-important first moment of truth isn't just happening in the store anymore. In fact, according to Google, it may not *ever* happen in the store anymore.

Google ZMOT

If any company were in a position to tell us about how people make purchasing decisions, it would be Google. The company powers the most widely used search engine on the planet and has a stated mission to help organize the world's information. They have a vested interest in looking at the science of human behaviour as well, considering over 90% of the company's revenue comes through their suite of tools for advertisers.

When Google's team looked at the work of P&G and studied the idea of FMOT, though, something didn't seem quite right. Their data

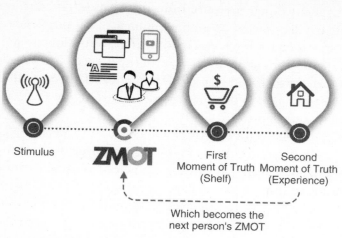

Figure 8.2 The Zero Moment of Truth

Source: Winning the Zero Moment of Truth, Google, Inc., 2011.

suggested that most consumers weren't seeing an ad and going straight into a retail store to consider purchasing and then buying an item. There was an intermediate step, and that step had everything to do with the web and with Google itself. Google's Vice President of Sales Jim Lecinski described this as a "grabbing-the-laptop moment" in an ebook he authored on Google's view of the importance of timing in retail and something they called the *Zero Moment of Truth* (ZMOT) (see Figure 8.2).

ZMOT was the real first step people took any time they saw an ad or a billboard, or someone walking down the street with a product they liked. *I wonder where she got that handbag?* ZMOT. *Is this Burger King the closest fast food or is there a Taco Bell around the corner?* ZMOT. *This restaurant menu looks good, but how do I know for sure?* ZMOT.

For any decision from looking for a new house to buying ballpoint pens, Lecinski wrote, "The buying decision journey has changed." Thanks to vast amounts of information and reviews on the web, as well as better mobile technology that allows us to get that information much faster, the moment when the buying decision is made is fundamentally shifting.

The conclusion of the report was clear. For anyone selling or buying anything, timing is critical; because if you don't reach a consumer exactly at that moment when they need the information that will influence their purchasing process, you will lose the sale.

Why Timing Is So Tough

There are only a few examples like Gilt.com where the timing is perfect and the whole system works. In most cases, the main problems with timing is that it is very hard to get it right for four important reasons:

1. **Audiences can require different timing.** Sometimes when you are trying to influence people to believe something, the timing can vary from person to person. This makes it very hard to deliver a message or a point of view that will influence multiple people at the right moment.
2. **Timing is hard to estimate in the moment.** There is a reason why people say hindsight is 20/20, and it is because of timing. It is very hard sometimes to understand whether you are in the right moment to make something happen or if you need to wait, because you don't have the benefit of perspective or time to analyze the situation. As a result, most of us make snap judgments and do the best we can with what we've got.
3. **Sometimes timing can change instantly.** Related to the last point, sometimes the right moment can come up quickly and without warning. It means that you need to be flexible enough to act in an unexpected moment, before an opportunity is quickly lost.
4. **Obvious timing creates more competition.** Planning for the right moment can be relatively obvious, and therefore create more competition. Every politician is going to advertise in the 48 hours before a vote. It doesn't make it the wrong timing, but sometimes the ideal timing for your message will also be the ideal timing for your competition—making it tougher to stand out.

More than anything else, having the right timing can often be a matter of experience or instinct to be able to spot the right moment to make something happen. This doesn't mean that you need to resign yourself to hoping you get lucky, though. There *is* a way to think about timing that can help you find the right moments more consistently than your competition.

The Three Elements of Timing

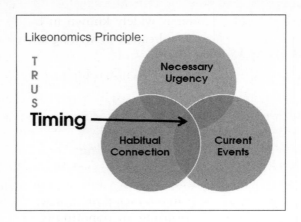

When the United Nations Summit on Climate Change, which was profiled in Chapter 5, was complete, critics who were disappointed with the results pointed to a lack of urgency as a critical reason why the talks had stalled. When it comes to timing, having a built-in sense of urgency is crucial as the first element, because it lets people know that something is important in the moment when you are trying to influence them to care.

Necessary Urgency	Habitual Connection	Current Events
The first element in getting timing right is having a built-in sense of urgency so it is clear that someone needs to act or pay attention *in the moment* that matters.	The best timing will connect your message or idea to a habit that the people you are trying to influence already have.	There are plenty of external factors that can influence getting timing right, so linking something to current events can only help with relevance.

If the focus of relevance is getting someone to care right now, the value of having the right timing is that it can help to *make it urgent.* Harvard Professor John Kotter is widely known in business circles as the *change guru.* His 18 books and career of writing and thinking have influenced how companies of all sizes manage the process of change. In 1996, he published his most well-known book, *Leading Change.* In it, he first described his signature eight-step process for implementing successful transformations. Step one in that process was always to create a sense of urgency. "Without a sense of urgency," he shared, "people won't give that extra effort that is often essential."[4]

But urgency alone is not enough. In order to build on having a sense of urgency, you also need to get as close as you can to a quality that may seem impossible to plan for: luck. Often, when people describe having the right timing for realizing an opportunity or just being in the right place at the right time, they use the word *luck* to describe the effect. As much as I might wish for a magic button to be able to predict and create luck, the probability of that ever occurring is unlikely.

Instead, you can put yourself in situations where you are *more likely* to have luck happen to you, which leads to the second element of timing: creating a habitual connection. Habit is a powerful force that explains much of what we do on a subconscious level without even thinking about it. Great timing means connecting with the habits people already have.

The final element has everything to do with the world around you, and the current events in it. It is a common lens that PR people use when they consider how to pitch a story to a reporter. In 2011, PR guru David Meerman Scott coined the term *newsjacking* to describe a method of PR where you pay attention to the largest stories in the news media and then find a way to hijack that story by adding another on top of it.

While it may seem opportunistic—this is ultimately the point. Sometimes having the right timing means taking the chance when it comes. Ultimately, though, timing is so important to whether you are able to be believable or not that it can easily mean the difference between success and failure.

CHAPTER SUMMARY
THREE THINGS TO REMEMBER ABOUT TIMING

1. The best ideas sometimes fail because of bad timing. Timing can be the secret ingredient that explains unexpected success, or unexpected failure.
2. While timing used to be a set variable (you either had it or you didn't), this has changed with today's time-shifting culture. Now, people can shift experiences to have them at times more convenient to them, which has made timing more important than ever.
3. A big part of timing has to do with relating something to the world around it. This is the same principle at the heart of effective PR efforts when a message relates to stories that are already being written on a topic.

Online Workbook and Action Guide:
How To Achieve The Perfect Timing

www.likeonomics.com/timing

Conclusion

In May of 2009 the business magazine Portfolio assembled a panel of professors from top business schools to create a Top 20 list that no executive wanted to be on. Their task was to comb through history and find the worst American CEOs of all time. Going back over 150 years, they looked at tales of corporate failure and greedy executives from many time periods. Coming in at #1 was Lehman CEO Dick Fuld who inspired hatred from all corners of the world for defending his own $484 million salary while Lehman was going through the largest bankruptcy in U.S. history ($613 billion in debts outstanding).

Way down at number 6 was a man from a different time who probably deserved to be #2. In his career as a corporate executive, Al Dunlap had several nicknames ... but the most popular was "Chainsaw Al." His specialty was firing people. Lots of people. A few months after he became CEO of kitchen appliance maker Sunbeam in 1996, he fired half of their 12,000 employees. At the time, it was the largest workforce reduction by percentage in corporate history.

Unapologetic, he wrote about his methods in his first book, which he titled *Mean Business*. One of his favorite sayings was, "If you want a friend, get a dog." The pleasure he seemed to take in firing people even inspired author Jon Ronson to interview Dunlap in 2010 while researching his book *The Psychopath Test*. Though Dunlap narrowly missed the mark for being a true psychopath by psychological standards, he showed many of the same tendencies (manipulative, superficially charming, lacking empathy, etc.).

In his time, Dunlap's "mean business" was seen by Wall Street not as a sign of psychotic behavior, but as the mark of a gifted "turnaround artist." If Jim Sinegal's insistence on treating Costco employees and customers fairly drove Wall Street crazy. Dunlap was their biggest darling. When he first took over at Sunbeam, the stock price rose over 50 percent overnight. It didn't last. In a matter of years, he was fired and the company would go bankrupt.

Perhaps the most telling part of Dunlap's entire story was the reaction of his own family to the news that he had been fired from Sunbeam. His estranged son Troy said, "I laughed like hell. I'm glad he fell on his ass." His only sister's reaction was worse. When interviewed by *BusinessWeek*, she shared that "he got exactly what he deserved."

It was short-term thinking that gave Al Dunlap his opportunities, and short-lived results were all he ever managed to deliver. In his path he left destroyed companies and livelihoods, fractured personal relationships, and lives today, as Ronson learned, as a sad and isolated man still deluded and convinced of his own self-worth.

The time where a business leader like Dunlap might have thrived, even for a short while, is over. Al Dunlap is a symbol of everything in the world that doesn't work anymore. He is also part of the reason why I wrote this book. We are in a new era of business, and that is good news for all of us.

Living in the Era of Likeonomics

The big idea of this book is that being more believable requires making personal connections, building relationships and finding a way to be more likeable. In my writing, the biggest surprise was just how easy it was to find examples of Likeonomics in action. It is all around us. People talk about how they got their current job because of a chance encounter with someone in their personal network. More and more marketing and advertising focuses on the idea of "brand humanity." Companies actively focus on how to show a more human (and humane) face to their customers.

Mega deals like the sale of Zappos to Amazon for $1.2 billion are widely seen by analysts as investments in corporate culture rather than hard technology or supply chain assets. The fact is, culture itself has become an asset. The way we value what matters and what works needs to shift. Spreadsheets don't explain our world, and the only way to create meaning from data is to look deeply at its context.

Throughout Likeonomics we saw examples of individuals and organizations who made powerful connections with others in unexpected ways. Chitta Mallik and his partner managed to forge a strong enough relationship to land the #1 NFL draft pick as a client. Scott DiGammarino took a failing regional Financial Advisor office and turned its fortunes around for more than a decade through his ability to inspire his staff. Oprah became the most influential woman in the world through her ability to constantly share the entire unfiltered truth with her audience. Dan Roam launched a revolution in business through his new ideas on the power of visual thinking to simplify challenges. And Nelson Mandela inspired his nation through his uncanny ability to get people talking over tea.

What do all of them have in common? They all used likeability on some level to achieve their success. The most important ideas in our world don't have to be the most complicated. The more complicated the problem, the more important it is to find simplicity in a solution. Finding a solution to the negativity that many people associate with capitalism today is a big challenge. Encouraging politicians to be more honest and forthcoming in an election year is a big challenge.

The big idea of this book is that there is a solution, and it comes down to likeability. Making the right connection from person to person can change everything. As a final reminder of how, I will take one last opportunity to share a short story with you about a man you will recognize, no matter where in the world you grew up.

Likeonomics on Mulberry Street

It was 1937 and a dejected cartoonist and author was about to burn his first manuscript. He never planned to be a writer, much less a cartoonist. He had actually gone to Oxford to become a professor, and most likely would have succeeded if he hadn't met a young American fellow student named Mary Palmer.

It was one day soon after they had met that she noticed him doodling in his notepad during class. Seeing his talent, she suggested he become an artist instead of a professor. It was like a light bulb had gone off. He not only took her advice, but soon fell in love and decided to marry her. It was only a matter of months before they decided to take a trip that would change both of their lives forever.

That summer they boarded the Swedish luxury ship *Kungsholm* and set sail for Europe from the New York Harbor. On the way back, as the story goes, he was on the upper deck, mesmerized by the monotonous sounds of the ship's engines. Inspired, he sat down with a few sheets of the ship's stationery and started writing the story that came into his head about a young boy who dreams up an elaborate story of imaginary people and vehicles traveling along Mulberry Street to tell his father, but ultimately tells him the truth instead.

It was his first book idea. Armed with the title "A Story No One Can Beat," he went out to try and sell the book to publishers. He was rejected 27 different times, all of which led him to that moment in 1937. Angry and defeated, he was ready to return home, burn the manuscript and give up. Little did he know that everything was about to change.

Walking home that moment he bumped into a college friend who, as chance would have it, had just accepted a new job just a few months earlier at Vanguard Press, a division of Houghton Mifflin. His friend agreed to share the manuscript and illustrations with a few executives. Vanguard agreed almost instantly to publish it, as long as he changed the title and was open to publishing under his assumed cartoonist pen name.

So it was that in 1937 an artist named Teddy Geisel, with the pen name Dr. Seuss, published his first book, *And to Think That I Saw It on Mulberry Street*. On the 75th anniversary of the publication of the book this year, NPR did a radio story on Dr. Seuss that ended with an interesting conclusion from the director of a museum that collects Dr. Seuss' works today. "If he had been walking down the other side of the street, he probably would never have become a children's author."

Life is full of unexpected meetings like this. More than anything else, this explains the power of Likeonomics. In a world where the difference between success and failure sometimes comes down to just being on the right side of the road, likeability is everything.

PART III

The StoryBook

Introduction: How the StoryBook Works

It is no accident that this section comes right after the tale of one of the most gifted storytellers in history. Now that we have taken the journey together through the idea and principles of *Likeonomics*, I have only one mission left to fulfill . . . inspiring you to act!

If you are going to take the lessons in this book and really apply them to your own life and career—the most powerful motivating force to help you get started is real stories. That is what this section and its collection of companion stories online aim to deliver.

In the following pages you will find tales of people, countries, and organizations both large and small who have achieved all kinds of success. I wish I could tell you that this book contributed to their success, but the truth is that it is rather the opposite. Their stories, and the dozens more like them at www.likeonomics.com/storybook are the real inspiration for this book.

These stories are the real, living heart of the idea behind *Likeonomics*. I hope you find as much inspiration in them as I have.

Bhutan—The Real Happiest Place on Earth

Industry: Tourism

The Story

There are only eight pilots in the world who are licensed to land an Airbus 319 in Bhutan. The isolated country is one of the world's most remote places, hidden in the eastern Himalayas between India and China. The country is also heavily influenced by their national religion of Buddhism, which has led to a rather surprising tourism policy.

In order to visit Bhutan, any tourist must pay a daily fee of $200, which covers guides and basic transportation. The policy is meant to encourage only *high-end* tourism and reduce the annual volume of tourists who visit the country. On the surface, this may seem like an odd thing to do. After all, why would any country want to limit tourists?

Bhutan, however, uses a different metric to make decisions. *BusinessWeek* magazine once rated Bhutan as the happiest country in Asia and the eighth happiest in the world. The government measures its citizens' gross national happiness (GNH) in much the same way that other countries measure gross domestic product (GDP).

No national policy is passed without first going through the happiness test to see if it will add to the GNH or take away from it. Cigarettes and plastic bags are banned, as neither is seen to be adding to the GNH. In addition, every citizen is given land by the government and the culture is one of extreme gentleness.

Their tourism policy has meant that more than 90 percent of the people coming to Bhutan are over 56 years old. But the tourism industry in Bhutan has no problem with the numbers as long as they avoid the fate of their neighbor to the North—Tibet.

Tibet has been plagued not only by the tension of its relationship with China, but also by an influx of what some Bhutanese describe as "pot smoking, pennypinching backpackers" who care little for the environment and create a more selfish and disrespectful tourism culture. It is something Bhutan wants desperately to avoid. For the Bhutanese, it is not about the backpackers as much as the volume. In 2010, just over 40,000 tourists visited Bhutan (compared with over 600,000 who visited Nepal).

Bhutan will never have an ambition to become a destination for the masses—nor will they focus on bringing everyone to see their country. For the citizens of the country, that is just fine. After all, in one of the happiest countries in the world, they may already have everything they need.

Why Is It an Example of Likeonomics?

In an industry where it is common to see people trying to be everything to everyone, Bhutan stands out for the **simplicity** of their approach. The country makes decisions based on the single **unselfish** metric of the happiness of its citizens. While many countries have adopted a "profit at any cost" mentality when it comes to attracting tourists, the **timing** of Bhutan's approach helps them to be unique.

Green Bay Packers—Why Cheeseheads Rule the NFL

Industry: Sports

The Story

The city of Green Bay in Wisconsin would be a small home even for a minor league baseball team. The fact that a major NFL franchise like the Green Bay Packers is based there might seem like a full blown mystery. Given the number of larger cities in the United States who might support a team in the most popular sport in the country—why Green Bay?

The simple reason is because back in 1919, when the Packers team was first founded, it was common for small cities to have NFL teams. Green Bay happens to be the only one of the small city teams to survive. And they are much smaller than the competition. Green Bay is the smallest market in the NFL, with a population of just a little over 100,000 people.

Their long history also means that they have a structure unlike any other team in the NFL. While most teams have individual owners who are usually billionaires and businessmen, the Packers are owned by the people of Green Bay—fans known as "Cheeseheads," named after the famed Wisconsin cheeses and their choice of headgear. People hold shares in the team, and while those shares are never worth any real money; they are a source of pride for the community. Thanks to the community ownership, the team also operates under different rules than the rest of the league.

While teams like the Dallas Cowboys or Washington Redskins are "cash cows," minting money through the sales of corporate stadium suites and team branded merchandise, most smaller teams work to build their own followings. To equal the playing field, the NFL has revenue-sharing programs to distribute money from TV licensing deals evenly to all the teams, but the NFL at its heart has always been a money-making business, with wealthy owners making millions from fans' passion for their teams and the game.

In contrast, the average ticket for a Packers game is still less than $100 (significantly less than other teams), and they have a policy of not overcharging their fans. Their approach makes them one of the only teams in the NFL who manage to win without overcharging their fans. And they do win.

The team has won 13 league championships, more than any other team in NFL history. In the 2011 season, they won the Super Bowl and were a championship team again in the 2012 season. More importantly, they are one of the most beloved teams in the league. The Super Bowl trophy is even named after their most famous coach—Vince Lombardi.

Why Is It an Example of Likeonomics?

Despite being based in the NFL's smallest market, the Green Bay Packers win legions of loyal fans because the team, its ownership, and the entire philosophy of the operation realizes the **unselfish** value of treating their fans fairly and authentically telling them the **truth** about the economics behind football instead of just making money from them. By also involving fans in the ownership of the team, they manage to build a **relevance** that is hard for other teams to match.

Khan Academy— Flipping the Rules of Education

Industry: Education

The Story

When a family member tells you that she prefers watching you on a YouTube video to actually hearing you in person, most people might take that as an insult. But Sal Khan isn't like most people. After earning three degrees at MIT and an MBA from Harvard, he started a job as an overqualified hedge-fund manager making seven figures a year. He had been a math whiz as well as a gifted student, and so he was also the first one that his younger family members would turn to when they needed someone to help explain their homework.

When his cousin Nadia asked for math help, to save time he started tutoring her over the Internet. He created a series of math videos to explain complex ideas to her in simple ways. Much to his surprise, those videos started getting a lot of views. Could math videos really go viral?

It turned out people need help understanding math—and not just kids either. Adults who go back to school, high schoolers who need a refresher on things they should have learned earlier in school but either forgot or never really learned properly ... each was an audience for Khan's videos. His no-nonsense style of simplifying math problems into shorter lectures that finally allowed people to "get it" were a hit. Pretty soon he started to branch out, creating more videos to simplify other math, science and business topics. His gift was his ability to explain complicated topics step by step.

One of the people who started using the site was Microsoft founder Bill Gates, who had been recommended to Khan's videos by a colleague and even used them to explain math concepts to his own kids. Impressed, he mentioned the site during a speech he was giving to an audience of hundreds of people. And then his Gates Foundation gave Khan a grant of $1.5 million to expand his online videos. Overnight, the Khan Academy began to get a lot of attention.

Today the site has more than 2,700 videos on topics as wide ranging as matrix vectors in linear algebra to price elasticity in microeconomics. What makes his videos so popular, apart from their simplicity? On the site, Khan offers the best description of why the site has been such a force for revolution in how people learn:

> *I teach the way that I wish I was taught. The lectures are coming from me, an actual human being who is fascinated by the world around him. The concepts are conveyed as they are understood by me, not as they are written in a textbook developed by an educational bureaucracy. Viewers know that it is the labor of love of one somewhat quirky and determined man who has a passion for learning and teaching. I don't think any corporate or governmental effort—regardless of how much money is thrown at the problem—can reproduce this.*

And so far, no one has.

Why Is It an Example of Likeonomics?

Learning from Sal Khan's videos is an experience in one-to-one learning from a teacher who never actually appears in front of you, but instead is **unselfishly** adding to the world's knowledge. He is believable because he takes complicated topics and makes them **simple** to understand. The videos are immediately **relevant**, because they are available on demand and usually used in conjunction with some schoolwork or other project.

Maverick Adventures—Kitesurfing with Richard Branson

Industry: Internet/Tech

The Story

There are some entrepreneurs who are in it to make money. Their definition of being an entrepreneur is creating the next multimillion-dollar idea, and then selling it and moving to the next thing. And then there's Yanik Silver. He writes blog posts about ideas that he has for helping his kids, who are four and six years old, learn about entrepreneurship. He organizes events called "Dangerous Dinners" where he invites people in his network to gather for absinthe tastings and other memorable experiences. His most ambitious goal is to inspire 1 million young entrepreneurs between the ages of 13 and 23 to start or grow their own business by 2020. And along the way, he has also built several seven-figure Internet businesses.

It's not a bad result for a lifelong entrepreneur who started his career at 14 years old selling latex gloves to medical facilities as part of his family business. What he learned early in his career was that the more you can offer to help others become successful, the more that success comes back to you. Perhaps the best example among his many efforts of this is his Maverick1000 network, which is made entirely of entrepreneurs who fit three simple criteria:

1. You must be a successful business owner with a minimum gross revenue of $1 million (which is verified).
2. You must be willing to share your business secrets openly.
3. You must *not* have a huge ego.

The network includes such visionary participants as X-prize creator Dr. Peter Diamandis, best-selling author and entrepreneur Tim Ferriss, and CEO of Joie de Vivre boutique hotel group Chip Conley. The network's most famous member, however, is also the one Silver works with to create his most memorable and sought-after event of the year.

The destination for this exclusive event is Necker Island, Richard Branson's private getaway. And the cost to attend? It is $40,000, which is donated to Virgin Unite (the nonprofit foundation of Branson's Virgin Group). Investment aside, it is a chance to get to know Branson himself.

During the week, Branson spends time with the entrepreneurs who attend and shares his thoughts. He goes kitesurfing and even taught one of the participant's daughters to swim this year. It is just another example of Yanik Silver doing what he does best; bringing entrepreneurs together to help them collectively change the world.

Why Is It an Example of Likeonomics?

By taking the role of a connector to bring successful entrepreneurs together, Yanik Silver manages to support entrepreneurs with **relevant** information and connections to help them achieve their ambitions. **Timing** is also a critical part of how he makes an impact, by offering entrepreneurs support in that crucial moment when an idea can succeed or fail. The organizations that he has started work because he encourages entrepreneurs to generously and **unselfishly** share their time and advice.

Anupy Singla— The Fast Rise of Slow Cooking

Industry: Publishing/Cooking

The Story

Anupy Singla is not your usual celebrity chef. She doesn't wear a big white hat or sell a signature line of cookware. She often tells her audience not to worry so much about measuring every ingredient with NASA-like precision. She doesn't have her own restaurant, or even aspire to. In fact, before writing her first cookbook, her "day job" was delivering the morning news on television.

After 10 years as an award-winning print journalist and broadcast TV anchor in the Chicago area, she decided to refocus on her kids and her real first love: cooking. Writing a cookbook had become an ambition for Anupy, and she had a unique idea to combine two popular topics together in a way that no one else had written about before—slow cooking and Indian food.

Writing a cookbook is all about deciding what to put in and what to leave out. Anyone who even considers it likely has hundreds of potential recipes to use. Anupy had the added complication of trying to teach people how to cook Indian food which can be complicated and vary widely in terms of how spicy people like to make it. So when she finally started writing the book, the first thing she did was start to test recipes.

On her blog she wrote about the recipes and started to build an audience of food enthusiasts. More importantly, she began to use Facebook to solve a fortunate problem that all this testing had caused . . . lots of extra food. Desperate for feedback, she started to offer free home cooked food to anyone who was willing to come by her house in Chicago with empty containers, as long as they promised to share a review about the recipe back with her. Throughout a year of testing, her best guess was that she must have fed about 300 Chicagoans.

Many of these people were fellow journalists—super connected and grateful for the great food to bring home to their families. Anyone who tried the food would share their feedback online and her virtual community of fans grew far beyond the few hundred she was able to feed in Chicago. By the time her book, *The Indian Slow Cooker*, launched, she had amassed a devoted following online.

On the day of her launch in September of 2010, the book shot to number one in the Indian Cookbook category on Amazon.com. More than 18 months later, it is still in the number one slot, an unheard of constant popularity in the rapid publishing world of cookbooks.

Since researching her recipes, Anupy also realized just how rare it was for the average household to have any of the spices on hand that most Indian food required. There was a secret weapon in this challenge, though, and it was something every Indian household already had. It was called the *masala dabba*—a large, round, stainless steel container that holds seven removable bowls, each meant for a different type of spice.

In 2011, she brought a prototype of her new "spice tiffin" design to a housewares show in Chicago. Two weeks later, thanks to a connection from an attendee at the show, they had a deal to sell the spice tiffin through Williams-Sonoma. The spice tiffin is selling well, and Anupy is already writing her second book, *Vegan Indian*, and once again offering up plenty of free food to local Chicagoans.

Why Is It an Example of Likeonomics?

Whether she is launching a best-selling book or landing a lucrative product distribution deal, Anupy Singla connects with her community by always offering up her **truthful** point of view as an author and a mom of two young daughters. She **unselfishly** offers to feed her readers in exchange for feedback and writes in a natural and **relevant** way to make Indian food approachable for people of any background.

The Backstory— The Making of *Likeonomics*

Writing a book is only partially about that moment when you ignore everything else and write. It is *everything else* that makes it a life-encompassing experience that relatively few people complete. In my case, it included months of combing through thousands of pages of articles and studies to find the most useful research and stories.

Over six months, I purchased exactly 43 books online and in actual book stores (about two per week) about brain science, marketing, retail therapy, spirituality, behavioral economics, visual design, and entrepreneurial stories of everything from starting the Weather Channel to creating and launching one of the world's most popular games (Jenga).

The entire process was a little like jumping into a pit filled with colored balls—you know you're not going to drown, but sometimes it sure feels like it. With enough time and thinking, though, the patterns emerge and the flow for the story of the book slowly unfolds. But it takes a while.

One of the central ideas of this book is that unexpected honesty offers a valuable way to help yourself or your organization be more believable. One way I want to do that is to give you an even deeper look into how this book came together.

To see it, you can visit: www.likeonomics.com/backstory.

There you can read uncorrected chapter drafts, the original proposal for the book, hand drawn visuals ideas that didn't quite make the final edit, and lots more. It is a chance for me to give you an inside look at what went into creating this book.

Whether you might one day choose to write your own book, or just want to peek behind the scenes, I invite you to join me for a journey behind the scenes of the making of *Likeonomics*.

www.likeonomics.com/backstory

Special Thanks

Special thanks to:
My amazing wife, Chhavi, for all her love and daily inspiration.

Rohan and Jaiden, for letting Daddy finish his "second chicken book."

My parents, Vinay and Nimmi, for their constant belief in me and the book.

Elizabeth Marshall and Jinal Shah for all their help in making the book itself as strong as it could be with editing support and continual smart thinking.

Steve Hanselman, my agent, for first offering the title of *Likeonomics*, and being a sounding board.

The rest of my family for all their help and thinking throughout.
and
The Likeonomics Curator's Network for bringing Likeonomics to life in a real and tangible way every day through their stories and contributions.*

---

*This could include you! If you are interested in joining The Likeonomics Curator's Network, visit www.likeonomics.com/curators to learn more about it.

Notes: Further Reading and Research

Author's Note: Throughout *Likeonomics* I have included numbered endnotes to offer a source for particular pieces of data or quotes that were used. As with any book, there were some sections where I didn't include notes only because it can very distracting to have five numbered notes on every page. You will find many of the references below, but a more complete list of the resources used (all indexed by chapter) is available at www.likeonomics.com/endnotes.

At this site you will be able to see images and articles about the stories included in the book, as well as highlights and quotes that I wasn't able to incorporate but will still be useful and interesting. And, perhaps most importantly, all of the links are clickable so you don't have to type in an insanely long link that might be mentioned here in the Notes section.

Prologue

1. www.wavian.com/blog/interviews/ana-free/.

Introduction

1. www.telegraph.co.uk/news/features/3634426/How-Nelson-Mandela-won-the-rugby-World-Cup.html.
2. www.bostonglobe.com/arts/books/2011/10/28/steve-jobs-walter-isaacson/6pEq4xP71Ht4Ha64auXhnO/story.html.
3. Matthew Symonds, *Softwar: An Intimate Portrait of Larry Ellison and Oracle*. Simon & Schuster, New York, 2004.

Chapter 1

1. Howard Zinn, *The Politics of History*, University of Illinois Press, 1990, p. 79.
2. Jonathan Rees, *Representation and Rebellion: The Rockefeller Plan at the Colorado Fuel and Iron Company*, 1914–1942, University Press of Colorado, Boulder, CO, 2010.
3. Martin Lindstrom, *Brandwashed: Tricks Companies Use to Manipulate Our Mind and Persuade Us to Buy*, Crown Business, New York, 2011.
4. www.gallup.com/poll/1597/Confidence-Institutions.aspx.

Chapter 2

1. Jim Collins, *Good to Great: Why Some Companies Make the Leap and Others Don't*, HarperBusiness, New York, 2001, p. 29.
2. Ibid., 30.
3. Source: National Golf Foundation.
4. Interview with Will Buckly in *The Observer*, "Mega Business Finds the Rough when Forging Links with Scotland," November 10, 2007.
5. Interview with Bill Storer in *Selling Power* magazine.
6. Keith Ferrazzi, *Never Eat Alone*, Crown Business, New York, p. 58.

Chapter 3

1. F. Mosteller, "The Tennessee Study of Class Size in the Early School Grades." *The Future of Children: Critical Issues for Children and Youths* 5, no. 2 (1995): 113–127.
2. Frederick M. Hess, "The New Stupid,"*Educational Leadership Journal* 66, no. 4 (December 2008/January 2009): 12–17.
3. Avinash Kaushik, *Web Analytics in an Hour a Day*, Sybex, Indianapolis, IN, 2007, p. 13.
4. ROI Institute website, www.roiinstitute.net.
5. Westen, Drew, *The Political Brain*, Public Affairs, New York, 2008, p. 422.

Chapter 4

1. *Newsday*'s Les Payne, www.oprahshowinfo.com/.
2. www.theroot.com/views/how-oprah-changed-television.
3. www.pbs.org/newshour/rundown/2011/05/the-oprah-phenomenon---by-the-numbers.html.
4. www.nytimes.com/1988/02/01/arts/donahue-vs-winfrey-a-clash-of-talk-titans.html.
5. www.paulekman.com/wp-content/uploads/2009/11/Newsletter_March091.pdf.

6. www.cultivatingemotionalbalance.org/?q=content/pilot-study.

7. David Kiley, *Getting the Bugs Out*, Wiley, New York, 2002, p. 99.

8. Robert Townsend, *Up the Organization*, Jossey-Bass, San Francisco, CA, 2007, p. 20.

9. James M. Kouzes and Barry Posner, "A Prescription for Leading in Cynical Times," *Ivey Business Journal* (July/August 2004).

Chapter 5

1. "Heroes of the Environment 2009 Issue," *TIME* (September 22, 2009).

2. http://robertmunsch.com/about.

3. Sebastian Mallaby, *The World's Banker*, Penguin Press, New York, 2004, p. 83.

4. Ibid., 388.

Chapter 6

1. www.ogilvy.com/News/Press-Releases/March-2010-In-Memoriam-Robyn-Putter.aspx.

2. Colin Mitchell and John Shaw, "What's The big ideaL?" Ogilvy Red Paper.

3. http://ethisphere.com/past-wme-honorees/wme2011/.

4. http://money.cnn.com/magazines/fortune/fortune_archive/2003/11/24/353755/index.htm.

5. Mary Midgley, *Evolution as Religion: Strange Hopes and Stranger Fears*, Routeledge, New York, 2002, p. 164.

6. Robert D. Putnam, *Better Together*, Simon & Schuster, New York, 2004, p. 4.

7. Don Tapscott, *Wikinomics*, Portfolio Hardcover, New York, 2006, p. 9.

8. Yochai Benkler, *The Penguin and the Leviathan*, Crown Business, New York, 2011, p. 13.

9. www.nytimes.com/2011/11/01/health/views/the-downside-of-doctors-who-feel-your-pain.html.

10. www.nytimes.com/2011/09/22/us/university-of-chicago-gets-42-million-gift-for-bucksbaum-institute.html.

11. Malcom Gladwell, *Blink*, Little Brown, New York, 2005, p. 40.

12. http://jama.ama-assn.org/content/277/7/553.abstract.

13. www.ncbi.nlm.nih.gov/pubmed/7911925.

14. William G. Pickering, "Kindness, Prescribed and Natural, in Medicine," *Journal of Medical Ethics* 23 (1997): 116–118.

15. www.physicianspractice.com/blog/content/article/1462168/1964496.

16. www.bbc.co.uk/news/magazine-12785802.

17. www.nytimes.com/2011/06/28/world/asia/28fukushima.html.

Chapter 7

1. www.fastcompany.com/magazine/148/how-ted-became-the-new-harvard.html

2. Interview with Steve Jobs, *BusinessWeek*, May 25, 1998.

3. http://blog.ted.com/2010/03/24/lets_simplify_l/

4. www.washingtonpost.com/opinions/pushing-the-government-to-speak-plainly/2011/11/18/gIQA7TmpLO_story.html

5. www.bbc.co.uk/news/10227680

6. Michele M. Asprey, *Plain Language for Lawyers*, Federation Press, New South Wales, Australia, 2010, p. 44.

7. http://pogue.blogs.nytimes.com/2011/06/02/flipping-to-grilled-cheese/#more-4131.

8. John Zerio, "Philips Sense and Simplicity," Case Study, Thunderbird School of Global Management.

9. www.newscenter.philips.com/main/standard/about/news/press/archive/2004/article-14535.wpd.

10. www.forbes.com/sites/maureenfarrell/2010/11/02/names-you-need-to-know-in-2011-john-maeda/

11. www.wethesavers.com/story/saving/

12. Arkadi Kuhlmann, *The Orange Code*, Wiley, Hoboken, 2009.

13. www.nytimes.com/2010/04/27/world/27powerpoint.html.

14. www.armedforcesjournal.com/2009/07/4061641.

15. Chip Heath and Dan Heath, *Made to Stick*, RandomHouse, New York, 2007, p. 46.

Chapter 8

1. David Price, *The Pixar Touch*, Vintage, New York, 2009, p. 142.

2. http://arbitron.mediaroom.com/index.php?s=43&item=467

3. www.sfgate.com/cgi-bin/article.cgi?f=/c/a/2012/01/05/BUS81MLA7C.DTL#ixzz1iyPJZ2D7.

4. www.zeromomentoftruth.com/google-zmot.pdf

5. John P. Kottler, *Leading Change*, Harvard Business Review Press, Cambridge, MA, 1996, p. 5.

**Visit www.likeonomics.com/endnotes to see
the full online endnotes.**

About the Author

Rohit Bhargava is a marketing expert focused on helping to bring more humanity back to business. He is the award-winning author of *Personality Not Included*, a book about using your personality to stand out, which has been translated into nine languages around the world. *Likeonomics* is his second book.

Rohit is a founding member of the world's largest team of social media strategists at Ogilvy, and Professor of Global Marketing at Georgetown University. His personal blog, "Influential Marketing" has been visited by more than 1 million unique readers, and has been rated one of the top 25 marketing blogs in the world.

Outside his consulting, teaching, and writing, he has been invited as a frequent keynote speaker at business and professional events such as TEDx and the World Communications Forum at Davos on personal success, marketing strategy, creative thinking, and why communications is no longer like feeding a baby. He lives in Washington, DC, with his wife, Chhavi, and two boys, Rohan and Jaiden.

For a visual bio, free ebooks, speaking samples, and daily marketing articles, visit hit site at www.rohitbhargava.com.

Index

Marketing (*continued*)
  corruptive force of, 12–14
  lies in, 15
Marlboro Man, 9–10
Marriott hotel, 27
Masala dabba, 162
Mass perception principle, 10–11
Mattis, James N., 123
Maverick Adventures, 159–160
McCain, John, 53
McChrystal, Stanley A., 123
McKinsey study, 21–23
Me-first consumerism, 90
Meaningful point of view, 85
"Measuring the ROI in a Cooperative
     Education Program," 50
Media
  impact of, 11
  PR use of, 5
  research, 139
Microsoft, 133–134
Midgley, Mary, 95
"Mild as May" slogan, 9
Mind and Life Institute, 62
Mitchell, Colin, 90
Mockler, Colman, 28
Monsters Inc., 134
Moon, Youngme, 40–41
Mosteller, Frederick, 45
Motion Picture Association of America
     (MPAA), 35
Motivation, 25
Mud Puddle (Munsch), 76
Mulberry Street, 147–148
Munsch, Robert, 76–78
Myhrvold, Nathan, 134

Nader, Ralph, 12
Nagari, Paolo, 78–80, 84
Nanny 911, 38
Nasheed, Mohamed, 73–75, 85
National Football League (NFL), 155–156
National Public Radio (NPR), 148
Natural disasters, 102–105
Natural language, 115, 128–129
Necessary urgency, 142
Necker Island, 160
Negativity, 11

Nestlé, 29
Networking, 34–36, 101–102
New England Journal of Medicine, 98
New York Times
  AVE coverage by, 54–55
  best-selling children's book list, 77–78
  coldhearted physician op. ed., 98
  Ludlow massacre coverage, 4–5
Newsjacking, 143
"The New Stupid," 46–47
Nike Plus system, 48
Niyikiza, Clet, 27
NOWNESS, 85–86

Obama, Barack, 53, 60
Observation, 51
"Occupy Wall Street," 7
Ocean's Eleven, 36
Offering value, 108
Ogilvy, David, 90
Ogilvy & Mather, 55
  big ideaL theory of, 90–91, 93
  global reach of, 93
  Putter reign at, 89–90
Okuyama, Ken, 120
opera "Operation Beautiful," 102
Oppenheimer, Daniel M., 114
"Oprah Effect," 60
The Orange Code, 122
Origin of Species (Darwin), 131
Originality, loss of, 39–40
Outsourcing, 40

Pairing, 135
Palmer, Mary, 147
The Paperbag Princess (Munsch), 77
Parker and Lee, 5
Patagonia, 92
Pennsylvania Railroad, 5
Pepsi-Cola, 38
"Pepsi Generation" slogan, 10
Personality Not Included (Bhargava), 16
Peters projection map, 132
Peters, Arno, 132
Philip Morris, 9
Philippines, 82–83
Philips, Jack J., 50
PhotoRealistic RenderMan, 133–134
Pickering, William G., 100